DISRUPTED URBANISM
Situated Smart Initiatives in African Cities

Nancy Odendaal

First published in Great Britain in 2023 by

Bristol University Press
University of Bristol
1–9 Old Park Hill
Bristol
BS2 8BB
UK
t: +44 (0)117 374 6645
e: bup-info@bristol.ac.uk

Details of international sales and distribution partners are available at bristoluniversitypress.co.uk

© Bristol University Press 2023

British Library Cataloguing in Publication Data
A catalogue record for this book is available from the British Library

ISBN 978-1-5292-1856-5 hardcover
ISBN 978-1-5292-1857-2 paperback
ISBN 978-1-5292-1858-9 ePub
ISBN 978-1-5292-1859-6 ePdf

The right of Nancy Odendaal to be identified as author of this work has been asserted by her in accordance with the Copyright, Designs and Patents Act 1988.

All rights reserved: no part of this publication may be reproduced, stored in a retrieval system or transmitted in any form or by any means, electronic, mechanical, photocopying, recording or otherwise, without the prior permission of Bristol University Press.

Every reasonable effort has been made to obtain permission to reproduce copyrighted material. If, however, anyone knows of an oversight, please contact the publisher.

The statements and opinions contained within this publication are solely those of the author and not of the University of Bristol or Bristol University Press. The University of Bristol and Bristol University Press disclaim responsibility for any injury to persons or property resulting from any material published in this publication.

Bristol University Press works to counter discrimination on grounds of gender, race, disability, age and sexuality.

Cover design: Qube Design
Front cover image: © Nancy Odendaal

To Vanessa Watson (12 October 1950 to 15 September 2021), mentor and friend, who inspired and enabled me to understand African cities on their own terms.

Contents

List of Figures		vii
List of Abbreviations		viii
Acknowledgements		x

1	**Introduction: Fantasies, Hope and Compelling Narratives**	**1**
	Introduction	1
	Thinking about disruption	2
	The African smart city	4
	The African city	8
	Finally	15

2	**The Expansive Nature of Platforms**	**17**
	Introduction	17
	Smart versus platform urbanism	20
	Space, agency and platforms	25

3	**Hacking Mobility**	**33**
	Introduction	33
	SafeBoda	36
	Disruption from within	40
	Relational disruption	43
	Conclusion	46

4	**Digital Food Dialogues**	**49**
	The travels of a banana	49
	Food security in African cities	51
	Optimizing the value chain: Twiga and Yebo Fresh	54
	Food security across space: community action networks	59
	Back to source: technology from above	65
	Conclusion	67

5	**Cyborg Activism**	**70**
	Introduction	70
	Cyborg activism in Cape Town, South Africa	73
	Knowledge generation as activism	81
	Elevated perspectives	83
	Conclusion	85
6	**Platform Practices and the Public Imagination**	**88**
	Introduction	88
	On (re)claiming the public sphere and embracing citizenship in the everyday	90
	Afrofuturism's significance as a cultural practice	99
	Culture as repair and practice	103
	Conclusion	104
7	**Conclusion: On Understanding Situated Platform Urbanism**	**106**
	Disrupted African cities: an introduction and a conclusion	106
	The many textures of African platform urbanism	109
	On disruption and hopeful futures	125

Notes	127
References	130
Index	141

List of Figures

3.1	*Boda-boda* riders waiting for a ride	37
3.2	A *boda-boda* stage in Kampala	39
4.1	Food sales and deliveries in Kibera, Nairobi	55
4.2	Twiga application marketing	56
4.3	Yebo Fresh marketing	59
4.4	Sinani voucher information	63
4.5	Urban farming in Gugulethu, Cape Town, in the shadow of a Shoprite supermarket	64
5.1	Ndifuna Ukwazi vacant land release campaign on Instagram	78
5.2	Lake Michelle and Masiphumelele, Cape Town	84
6.1	Kibera security map in situ	93

List of Abbreviations

4IR	Fourth Industrial Revolution
AFSUN	African Food Security Urban Network
ANT	actor–network theory
API	application programming interface
CAN	community action network
CBD	Central Business District
CEO	chief executive officer
COO	chief operations officer
CSO	civil society organization
CTT	Cape Town Together
DPAK	Drivers and Partners Association of Kenya
FAO	Food and Agriculture Organization
FEDUP	Federation of the Urban Poor
GDP	gross domestic product
GPS	Global Positioning System
GSMA	Global System for Mobile Communications Association
GUFI	Gugulethu Urban Farming Initiative
HFIAS	Household Food Insecurity Access Scale
ICT	information and communication technology
ICT4D	information and communication technology for development
IoT	Internet of Things
K&T	knowledge and technology
KCCA	Kampala City Capital Authority
MIT	Massachusetts Institute of Technology
MNCs	multinational companies
MOCAA	Museum of Contemporary Art Africa
NU	Ndifuna Ukwazi
PSPP	Pul Slum Pan People
RFID	radio frequency identification
RtC	Reclaim the City
SDI	Shack/Slum Dwellers International

LIST OF ABBREVIATIONS

SLURC	Sierra Leone Urban Research Centre
STS	science and technology studies
UAV	unmanned aerial vehicles
UN	United Nations
WCEDP	Western Cape Economic Development Partnership

Acknowledgements

This manuscript was born in Johannesburg, South Africa, in 2020 as the realities of the COVID-19 pandemic became more apparent and global. During the conceptualization process, I want to acknowledge the inputs and support of Paul Stevens from Bristol University Press, who immediately acknowledged my vision for the book and its value – an essential reassurance for a first-time book author! Thank you to Roger Weiss, whose technical knowledge and emotional support in these early stages were invaluable, and my good friends Skye Dobson and Philippa Tumubweinee for their encouragement and insights.

Fortunately, I had done the necessary onsite fieldwork by March 2020. Here, I wish to acknowledge the kindness of my friend Katie Knight, who generously offered me a home in Kampala, Prince Guma in Nairobi, and whose insights provided me with a more textured view of digital appropriation in East Africa. I also wish to acknowledge the many respondents in Kampala and Nairobi that made time for discussions and explorations, in particular, Ricky Thompson, Baraka Mwau, Joy Mboya and Deepa Shekar. This onsite work was later expanded upon by many Zoom meetings and WhatsApp interviews, very much in line with the themes of this book. I am very grateful here to the respondents and the friends that put me in touch with them, in particular, Leeanne Brady, Marcela Guerrero Casas, Robyn Park-Ross, Michael Clark, Kyla Hazell and my colleagues associated with the Sierra Leone Urban Research Centre (SLURC).

It is very rare to be able to commit time solely to the writing of a book when employed as an academic. Staying motivated is largely due to background support from family, friends and colleagues. Special thanks in this regard to Welma Odendaal, Wilna Botha, Marion da Silva, John Morris, Tanja Winkler, Tania Katzschner, Janine Meyer and, posthumously, Vanessa Watson (to whom this book is dedicated). Thanks also to Alan Mabin, Cynthia Cross, Evan Blake, Ola Söderström, Alex Aurigi, Ayona Datta, Stephen Graham, Rob Kitchin, Andrea Pollio and Simon Marvin for their inputs over the years that have influenced this book. The 'Flamingals', my peer group of 'wild swimmers', kept me sane during the writing of this text through many swims in the cold Atlantic Ocean and squad training. I apologize in advance to others for inadvertently omitting their names and roles. Acknowledgement is also due to the University of Cape Town and the Vera Davie Foundation for funding support for travel and sabbatical.

1

Introduction: Fantasies, Hope and Compelling Narratives

Introduction

In 2017, I was invited to speak at a workshop in Calgary, Canada, on the African smart city. I found this to be a curiously ill-defined task given the size and diversity of the continent. The central message I hoped to convey was that the manifestation of digital technologies is intrinsically connected to people's livelihood strategies. What distinguishes African cities, if one is to generalize, are a number of features that colour the incorporation of information and communication technology (ICT) into city processes: informality, crumbling infrastructure and increasing urban poverty. These facts are not surprising, and this is not a new argument, but I nevertheless experienced some challenges to my presentation. My choice of projected images of street vendors using mobile phones and billboards promoting ubiquitous connectivity juxtaposed with immediate city surroundings showing dilapidated road infrastructure was an uncomfortable contrast to the smart city imaginary. Corporate displays of smart cities in Africa are eerie in their similarities: tall, glass-clad skyscrapers interspersed with wide avenues and slick inhabitants glued to their mobile phones. They portray a strange 'placeless-ness' that could be Dubai, Singapore or Seoul. Regardless of the imaginaries that inspire them, they bear very little resemblance to the 'real' city, in Africa or elsewhere.

At the same event, a colleague remarked on how my hometown, Cape Town, had a mythical quality to it, a Shangri-La of sorts: beautiful and historically and geographically compelling, perched on the Southern tip of Africa and thus geographically remote enough to reinforce this fantasy. I was reminded of yet another compelling narrative: Cape Town as the 'Silicon Cape', the 'Investment Connection into Africa' displayed on a billboard at Cape International Airport. It struck me that my research included many aspirations: the smart city, the connected citizen and, of course, innovation as central to African livelihoods. I appear to peddle in fanciful ideas, but

I believe it imperative to probe them and confront the contradictions contained therein.

The relationship between technology and social development has been subject to important areas of criticism that feature in a diverse range of disciplines: urban studies, development studies and urban geography are among them. In my early academic career, I was largely dissatisfied with the structural approaches often taken, where the hegemony of multinational technology and infrastructure producers is seen to determine local socio-technical agendas. Science and technology studies (STS) resonates because it is interdisciplinary and enables a relational frame of analysis that acknowledges the interface between technical and human agency. It opens the conceptual door to contextuality, embeddedness and inquiry into how technology travels and morphs in different places. Thus, this book is not about smart cities; on the contrary, it aims at disrupting many of the associations that surface when considering the interface between technology and African cities. It is ostensibly a book about hope, seeking to understand the subaltern and modest but powerful, digitally informed innovations that could potentially shift conditions for people living in African cities in a meaningful way. The aim is to explore how these are shaped and what impact they may have on people's livelihoods in urban spaces.

This book is essentially a journey across a number of places, both physical and digital. I explore initiatives in Nigeria, Sierra Leone, Uganda, Kenya and South Africa to determine how smart urbanism manifests when driven by Africans. These instances of technology appropriation are discussed as vignettes – examples used to inform an overall narrative on how digital platforms impact cities. They are based on a review of academic and grey literature, interviews with a number of respondents, the online perusal of web sites and social media, and a little netnography. The lens for my exploration is informed by the African urbanism literature – a recognition that cities on the continent have their own peculiarities and qualities that feature in both the online and the offline lives of their inhabitants. In this introduction, I discuss what these key concepts are, the rationale for my approach and the structure of the book. I start with the key theme of the title of this book – 'disruption' – and transition to explorations of the claims of African smart city initiatives and how they often contradict the realities of city life on the continent. These characteristics are introduced thematically as the structuring elements of the book.

Thinking about disruption

Using the term 'disruption' within the context of debates on smart cities in Africa is a risky endeavour. The word has become so loaded with promise that it is difficult to disassociate it from its neoliberal gloss, or to step away from its promise of technology nirvana or the mythical leapfrogging towards modernist emancipation. In some ways, the term lends itself to irony. While disruption in the platform economy has led to an entrenchment of the economic power and social influence of tech multinationals, a dictionary definition enables a broader enquiry, with the Oxford English Dictionary describing it as: 'a process that makes it difficult for something to continue in the normal way, or the act of stopping something from continuing in the normal way',[1] implying a disruption of the status quo. In other words, technology disruption could also be interpreted as, or, indeed, harnessed for, subversion.

In the business studies literature, the distinction is often made between 'incremental', 'radical' and 'disruptive' change (Dixon et al, 2018). Central is Christensen's theory of disruptive innovation, which implies substitution: extract firms replace incumbents with a technological solution that it more attuned to the market needs of a particular niche market. This application then expands in its influence, with research and development, as well as market exposure, to satisfy the requirements of the mainstream market (Danneels, 2004). In an urban setting, the term is often used in relation to digital platforms and associated concerns that multinational companies (MNCs), such as Airbnb and Uber, are undermining public governance – or, as a more positive interpretation, that they enable greater market agility and user satisfaction. The literature on this as an extension of urban infrastructure and a technology architecture that lends itself to reinvention is explored in more detail in Chapter 2. The interplay between public and private is often explored in the literature on platform urbanism and smart cities (Sadowski, 2020a; Söderström and Mermet, 2020; van Doorn, 2019), with the underlying anxiety about the power and influence platform MNCs exercise in everyday city governance and the impacts for citizens. This is an important debate and clearly needs to be taken seriously in resource-stretched environments. The spirit of this book is, however, that there is space for innovation and reinvention.

The issue of displacement is a necessary enquiry and cannot be ignored. With disruption comes fallout, and in marginal urban circumstances within African cities that are divided along income lines, this can be risky yet also pertinent in a context where state institutions are weak. What may be deemed disruptive is deeply contextual: innovation for one social group could be seen as part of the everyday by others, depending on functionality and familiarity (Dixon et al, 2018). The need to consider disruptive technological processes within policy and institutional arrangements is essential, and within a socio-technical framework, that would relate to the 'landscape' and 'regime' elements of a multi-scalar perspective (Dixon et al, 2018). My intention is to explore how technology-led processes from the bottom up lead to city processes not continuing as normal, that is, how they disrupt *the city*. While one conventional definition of disruption could be 'the process of distribution of innovations that are based on IoT [Internet of Things] and replacing existing market leaders and prevalent systems' (Roy et al, 2016: 200), my enquiry focuses on how 'business as usual' in the city is unsettled by technology innovation. Any such process takes into account social acceptance, technological awareness and consumer needs, seen as critical to 'cooperative design processes', in human–computer interaction language (Roy et al, 2016). By its nature, the notion of disruption lends itself to an interface with socio-economic realities – or it should. This is the central ethos of this book. Rather than seeing the producers of technology as central agents in their influence, the practices captured here are enacted and developed over time, and represent a distributed agency that could impact in ways contrary to what was intended. In many ways, this book is speculative, in that it explores possibilities for everyday knowledge production that responds to endogenous urban problems. Thus, it considers not only technology 'landings' in the African context, but also how different material realities can activate agency, sometimes in unexpected ways. Interpreting and knowing the material contextually opens up spaces where conversations about alternative socio-technical futures can happen.

There are many examples of socially outward-looking technology innovations that impact the city, for example, the combination of the IoT, cloud storage and 3D printing in healthcare and, of course, education. The COVID-19 pandemic has mainstreamed many of these as we applied technology to everyday problems by necessity. If you type 'disruption' or 'innovation' into Google or, indeed, Google Scholar, discussions of innovation hubs most often pop up. Mythical constructs, such as the 'Silicon Savannah' of East Africa (Nairobi) or, indeed, the case of Cape Town's reputation as the aforementioned 'Silicon Cape', are not only compelling, but also criticized as narratives that mask the true struggles and small appropriations that typify African urbanism (Guma, 2019; Odendaal, 2020). These accounts ignore how these corporate governance practices reinforce exclusionary macroeconomic narratives (Pollio, 2019). Technology disruption in African cities, like in other parts of the world, is contextually embedded and associated with structural legacies, as well as local livelihoods. This premise is in stark contradiction to the popular narrative of the African smart city.

The African smart city

The smart city narrative in Africa is more attuned to anticipated opportunities than problem solving, even though corporate language often claims that the smart city is a panacea for the difficulties that cities experience in relation to climate change and urbanization. As a discourse, the focus is on an envisioned future: technology-enhanced cities that provide flawless urban experiences unencumbered by the characteristics that are generally ubiquitous: traffic, informality and infrastructure disfunction. The language of 'world-class status' is an integral part of the smart city argument that drives such developments as Nairobi's Konza Tech City and Hope City outside Accra (Watson, 2015). These 'utopian imaginings' (Watson, 2015: 37) share very little detail on what the problems are to be solved or, indeed, how they aim to solve them. As Watson (2015: 37) eloquently points out, the rendered glass buildings, wide boulevards and irrigated gardens visually captured in artists' digital impressions would rely on basic water supply, uninterrupted power supply and maintenance regimes that are seldom available to the majority of African urban dwellers. Practically, the plans reveal futuristic representations that bear greater resemblance to Dubai and Singapore than Nairobi or Kigali. The marketing discourse overrides any attempt at stakeholder needs analysis, despite the claims to solve the multifaceted problems associated with rapid urbanization and climate change. In all of this, technology is promoted as possessing the agency to effect change. The problem is that these fantasies are often pursued by national governments together with property speculators and engineering and tech MNCs at the expense of basic services and infrastructure maintenance in existing cities.

The development of smart cities is not necessarily done in isolation from plans or public visions, however. In Nairobi, Kenya, for example, large-scale master-planned satellite cities that conform to the smart city tag are underpinned by the city's long-term development strategy ('Nairobi Metro 2030'), the national 'Vision 2030' and the country's ICT transformation roadmap (Guma and Monstadt, 2020). In South Africa, recent proposals for smart cities in Gauteng province and the Eastern Cape coast are driven by the country's embrace of the Fourth Industrial Revolution (4IR) as a solution to high degrees of joblessness and the decline in economic growth (Söderström et al, 2021). In Lagos, the construction of Eko Atlantic, a satellite city on reclaimed land off the coast of Victoria Island, claims to offer solutions for resilience and ecological reclamation, but its long-term impact for the residents of Lagos and its fragile ecosystem is in question (Ajibade, 2017). Konza Tech City in Nairobi is portrayed as a haven for businesses, away from the city's notorious traffic and therefore also a safe space for investment. As discussed by Guma and Monstadt (2020: 2), the value that drives these plans sees ICT as a developmental tool that can cure urban problems, contribute to entrepreneurial development and transform Nairobi into a 'Silicon Savannah'. Despite these intentions, the authors correctly claim: 'technological visions and techno-centred strategies are detached from the ways the majority of urban residents in Nairobi interacts with ICTs' (Guma and Monstadt, 2020: 2). Thus, the separation between public and private actors is not distinct in the envisioning of corporate smart cities; many national and local African governments are directly implicated in these utopian narratives. These are largely 'band-aid' interventions that do not engage the systemic issues that impact cities.

In many ways, the questioning of these initiatives foregrounds the notion of values and the roles played by normative constructs of what the ideal city should be, who it is for and what it should look like. As a visual narrative, the African smart city shares more with Dubai and Singapore than it does with any cultural reference to place and history evident in the messy and vibrant qualities that define the continent's urban spaces. The intention is not to over-romanticize messiness or lack of infrastructure; many suffer as a result of a lack of basic urban services. The issue relates to the contradictions that surface when one considers the smart city discourse in relation to the potential impact on ordinary livelihoods. What this encapsulates is a clash in values, as represented in different visions for the city: an ordered, predictable and modernist city driven by smart technology and artificial intelligence (AI), in contrast to aspirations towards inclusive, diverse urban spaces that articulate with the qualities and histories of place and the livelihood strategies employed to traverse them. Thus, the *actual* technology-mediated city in Africa looks very different, of course, from the visual imagery that accompanies such proposals. I have argued elsewhere that smart urbanism is largely 'in the making' as survival strategies interface with technology appropriation (Odendaal, 2020). Similarly, Prince Guma's (2019) work in Nairobi shows us that the relationship between utility infrastructures and digital technology is not a straightforwardly functional one, as poor communities in Nairobi find ways to repurpose electricity metering to fit their budgetary needs, while Baptista (2015) shows how closely tied smart metering systems are to household planning in her work on Maputo. What emerges from careful case-study research in these published cases is a mediated agency that represents a more relational unfolding, as opposed to that presupposed by the determinist rhetoric that underpins so many corporate representations of the African smart city.

New technologies are, of course, useful and increasingly critical to urban functioning. Infrastructural functions and connectivity impulses enabled by digital tools enable managed responses to climate crisis events and, more recently, the COVID-19 pandemic. With lockdown measures forming the centrepiece of COVID-19 pandemic national responses, the need for connectivity surfaced significantly during 2020, building on an exponential trend towards smartphone ownership on the continent. According to the Global System for Mobile Communications Association (GSMA), 45 per cent of the population in sub-Saharan Africa were subscribed to mobile phone services by 2020, with an anticipated 1 billion mobile connections anticipated in 2024. Many of the contributing factors to this uptake include corporate responses that acknowledge the need for agility and contextualized financial and technical mechanisms, such as the production of cheaper phones, including sub-US$100 devices from Chinese brands such as Tecno and Infinix, as well as the development of smart feature phones (CSM Association, 2020).

In the day-to-day survival strategies of urban dwellers in African cities, affordable access to hardware and data remains an issue. It is common for individuals to own multiple SIM cards, switching between them in order to take advantage of a particular network's deals or to maintain service when one network goes down. At the same time, if an individual does not own a phone, they may have access to someone else's. Initiatives that enable more granular payment schemes contribute to an increase in affordability. Kenyan company Safaricom's Lipa Mdogo Mdogo initiative, in partnership with Google's operating system partner Android, allows customers to access 4G Internet services through a smartphone that they can pay for as they use on a daily or weekly basis. The GSMA anticipates that the number of smartphone connections in sub-Saharan Africa will almost double to reach 678 million by the end of 2025, with an adoption rate of 65 per cent in 2020. The mobile phone is not only a critical piece of infrastructure, but also a node in the connectivity ecosystem that includes both material artefacts and the continuously emerging strategies employed to gain access within the limits of affordability. Key to an understanding of these strategies deployed towards greater connectivity is an analytical lens that allows for a socio-technical analysis in which material and human agency are recognized to be intertwined.

Corporate responses are, of course, about expanding markets, as are many master-planned smart cities, as Africa has become the 'next big market' for technology MNCs partnering with speculative property developers, often employing a 'rhetoric of urgency' (Datta, 2015: 5) as part of their promotional logic. This can be seen in the following quotation from management consultants (Deloitte & Touche, 2015: 6):

> Due to increased access to connectivity and the associated predicted urbanization, African cities are going to have to start focusing on what the city of tomorrow will look like. African cities are well positioned to leapfrog into the mid-21st century. Without the successful adoption and appropriate selection of technology, African cities will indeed be left behind as more and more Africans look for brighter futures on other continents.

These proposals problematize urbanization, citing the accelerated growth of African cities and lagging infrastructure investment within the context of the climate crisis as determining factors. There are, of course, varied experiences of urbanization across the continent and variation in growth rates, and in some instances, secondary cities are experiencing greater growth rates than primary cities (Potts, 2009). Connections to rural areas, circular migration and such spatial configurations as peri-urban fringe development are important factors to consider (Parnell and Pieterse, 2014). The concern that top-down state-led satellite city development potentially only serves the elites in cities with widespread poverty is very pertinent; however, perhaps more worrying, as mentioned earlier, is that such master-planned areas can exacerbate spatial and social inequalities, and further deepen infrastructure backlogs.

My aim in this book is not to simply add to the critical literature of smart cities, nor is it to idealize bottom-up approaches as examples of subaltern urbanism (as compelling as that may be). Rather, it is to present an argument that teases out the opportunities that emerge from the sweet spot between corporate ambitions and grounded innovations. The vignettes in this book are situated in a range of sectors, with ambitions that range from the ideological to the unapologetically commercial. This nexus is informed by the unique and variable circumstances that shape African urban spaces yet sometimes takes cues from MNCs in developing home-grown digital solutions to urban problems. In doing so, I hypothesize that the very nature of these challenges is defined, probed and delineated through a local lens that informs the way technology is appropriated. As Watson (2015: 37) correctly observes about corporate smart city visions: 'These plans completely ignore the quite obvious human and social dimensions of smart – the role of social capital and networks of trust and reciprocity that are prerequisites for innovation.' Thus, the task is not only to probe what such innovations look like, but also to surface the inherent qualities of African urban spaces that provide the canvas for disruptive brushstrokes.

The African city

The 'urbanization as problem' discourse embedded in many corporate smart city literatures is accompanied by a corporate view that the economic growth and agglomeration economies of cities represent opportunities for innovation and invention. In the African context in particular, it also represents challenges for city governments in terms of service provision through addressing infrastructure backlogs and responding to pressures for spatial expansion. The United Nations Human Settlements Programme (UN Habitat) predicts that by 2030, 50 per cent of the continent's population will be urban (UNDP, 2017). Placing the onus on government, the agency reinforces the urgency for African governments to enable service delivery and housing for these needs, recognizing that informal settlements are a reality that cannot be wished away. This is a message that contrasts the top-down technology-driven messages from ICT corporates that use the city agenda as a marketing backdrop. Both messages contain a sense of urgency and action, as well as a call to reform the distribution of resources and public spending. Also implicit is the fact that government alone cannot respond meaningfully to these challenges. Some of the problems are fiscal, with inadequate fiscal decentralization to local government, polarization, inequality and growth in informality as urban dwellers are increasingly unable to secure jobs and shelter in cities (UNDP, 2017).

The many assumptions that informed the early planning of African cities, were tied to Anglo-American experiences following the Industrial Revolution, where population growth was assumed to be accompanied by economic and employment growth. It appears that not that much has changed. Many spatial plans for African cities are prepared by international consultants that apply Northern concepts to contingent and often volatile urban environments. Top-down interventions assume political stability but overestimate the ability of the state to deliver. The predictable outcome is often a 'splintered urbanism' (Graham and Marvin, 2001), where master-planned neighbourhoods and new industrial and business districts are spatially disassociated from the everyday experiences of the majority of urban dwellers.

At the time of writing, during the COVID-19 pandemic, the circumstances that inform urban livelihoods have become particularly dire. COVID-19 risk factors are acute in African cities, in part, due to the largely unplanned and poorly managed urbanization process resulting in widespread informal settlements and severe infrastructure and service deficits. In 2019, about 47 per cent of Africa's urban population lived in slums or informal settlements, which translates into about 257 million people across the whole of Africa (UNDESA, 2019). Only 55 per cent and 47 per cent of Africa's urban residents have access to basic sanitation services and hand-washing facilities, respectively. Furthermore, most urban residents rely on the informal sector that employs 71 per cent of Africans, making them highly vulnerable to loss of income and unable to abide by restrictions and lockdown measures (UNDESA, 2019). African city centres are dense spaces with crowded public transport and marketplaces, making social distancing almost impossible. Infrastructure deficits and high densities in informal settlements, coupled with limited social and health services, have made African cities particularly vulnerable to such shocks as the pandemic.

Increasingly, African urban scholars from the North and South are calling for a global perspective that recognizes African urbanism as possessing embedded qualities, not simply incomplete versions of the ideal developed ('Western') city, shining an investigative lens on the many approaches and strategies employed by a diversity of stakeholders in the continuous redefinition of urbanity. In what Simone and Pieterse (2017) refer to as an age of 'dissonance', the boundaries in urban Africa between the global and the national, between the public and the private, and between the formal and the informal are increasingly blurred. Africa has always been global and has influenced the rest of the world as much as it has been shaped by it, producing different modes and models of 'worlding' (Roy et al, 2016) that are also distinctly local.

The ubiquitous presence of technology potentially reveals a local–global dynamic, now deepened through digital platforms. The question that informs this book is whether these platforms, as they are appropriated and harnessed locally, potentially enable substantive change. In order to explore this question, I focus on four challenging features of African cities that I would argue are ubiquitous throughout the continent, and I explore examples of technology disruption that respond, directly or inadvertently, to those challenges. The term 'disruption' is therefore used in a number of ways. In addition to the emphasis on practices that disrupt markets in the conventional sense, it is also used in two other ways: disrupting the distinction between local and global, or, indeed, Global South and North; and in the context of this book, disrupting the city and its systems.

The underlying thesis is that endogenous initiatives that harness smart technologies are emblematic of 'home-grown' solutions to urban problems largely unresolved by the state. These local answers to pressing needs are not indigenous in the pure sense; rather, they are locally evolved and initiated, despite often being informed and sometimes constrained by MNC technology. Here, I am inspired by the work done under the auspices of postcolonial STS, particularly Warwick Anderson's (2002: 649) statement that 'Science and technology are necessarily local practices, yet they can travel.' Some of the examples discussed in this book do, indeed, travel, but their landings are contingent upon many factors. Within this context, I would define the vignettes discussed as local disruptive socio-technical practices that respond to specific contextual needs. Thus, the significance is not so much the 'landings', but the social ecosystems and associational infrastructure that determine their ongoing functioning. The word 'appropriation' is one I often use to describe the agency displayed in repurposing, hacking and retooling digital tools to suit the immediate circumstances that inform urban life. In narrowing down the specific issues that are potentially open to digitally informed problem solving, I group these in accordance with the following themes: mobility, food security, urban activism and, finally, public life and imagination in African cities. These themes are not intended to give a comprehensive account of smart urbanism in relation to city systems. I would argue that they represent a range of qualities that speak to some of the most intractable challenges that impact cities and the future of urban spaces on the continent.

Mobility

Enter any African city from an airport or bus station and one's time budget needs to double given traffic and road conditions. For many, these frustrations translate into the everyday. Close to 15 per cent of Nairobi's population spend an average of four hours in traffic to commute to work, while a 10 km commute in Seoul takes just 21 minutes and in London only 40 minutes; in Nairobi, the same commute can take 1 hour and 18 minutes, nearly double the London figure (Civic Data Design Lab, 2019).

A core part of household mobility strategies for many African city-dwellers is the use of paratransit, that is, travel forms that fall between passenger travel modes and autonomous private transport. In a region where the informal economy absorbs as much as 80 per cent of the labour force in cities and where mobility systems are simply not keeping pace with city expansion, informal transport provides essential incomes and affordable mobility to many.[2] Paratransit plays an essential function in enabling the livelihoods of drivers and passengers (Behrens et al, 2015). These largely informal systems run concurrently with more formal means, which are woefully inadequate in many cases. Ride-hailing applications, such as Uber and Lyft, have not only found captive markets in cities such as Nairobi, Cape Town and Dar es Salaam for middle- to upper-income passengers, but also provided opportunities for income for drivers. Chapter 3 commences with a general view on how digital disruption has impacted the mobility sector (Uber, LittleCab and Lyft) and how it is manifested in African cities. There is a debate about the extent to which locals benefit from these apps, despite Uber's claims that it is, for example, inherently developmental.

The needs and parameters of the paratransit sector are therefore central to understanding mobility. The first empirical vignette, SafeBoda, follows the development of a home-grown app for the safe and efficient use of *boda-bodas*, that is, motorcycle taxis, which form the backbone of public transportation in Kampala, Uganda and many other African cities. Discussion of this example will reveal a number of themes that relate to the purpose of the book, for example, the value of networks across transportation options as part of an economic ecosystem (another example is Sendy, a Kenyan start-up that is essentially an app-based delivery service), as well as insight into how these platform-based interventions can enable livelihoods, for example, SafeBoda connects users with informal food producers (*Kya'kulya Chakula*), which was an important function during the COVID-19 pandemic. Also included is a discussion of rider-owned or cooperative ride-hailing apps, such as BebaBeba in Kenya. The labour dimensions are important given the unstable conditions for workers in such marginalized circumstances. Also of interest is how the development of these applications were social and technical processes. Relations of trust and the connections that are enabled between actors through technology deployment point to a material–human interface that evolves in response to geographic and temporal contexts. Contingency as a function of flow and connection is one of the themes that emerges from many of the examples in this book, and it will be discussed more comprehensively in the conclusion.

Food security

Food security is central to understanding how the informal economy forms part of the food value chain and how rapid urbanization undermines urban food production. Access to adequate nutrition is as much a function of governance and planning as it is about the physical availability of markets and shops. With climate change and the phenomenon of climate refugees, the ability of cities to enable food distribution will become particularly urgent. The empirical vignettes in Chapter 4 will begin with a recap of the value of informal food production networks and their enrolment into digital platforms. The initial focus is on the food value chain and its inefficiencies in relation to food security. The first story is of Twiga in Nairobi, an application that connects small-scale farmers with informal food vendors. The firm has grown substantially and has plans for expansion into other parts of the continent, but its Kenyan operations illustrate the importance of urban infrastructure in relation to food distribution and the role that the platform economy can play in enabling efficiencies for large- and small-scale producers.

In Cape Town, South Africa, lockdown measures during the first wave of the COVID-19 pandemic had severe implications for informal food sellers and food security in general. The inefficiencies of the urban system and the spatial inequities still inherent in this post-apartheid city became apparent as the distribution of food was only open to large commercial suppliers. Many charities and non-governmental organizations (NGOs) stepped in to distribute food parcels. A second vignette focuses on Cape Town Together (CTT), an umbrella group that facilitated the formation of community action networks (CANs) in the city's neighbourhoods. Using social media and WhatsApp group functioning, there were 170 CANs in the city at one point, focusing on building community and enabling food access. Each CAN is different and responds to its local milieu appropriately. Some expanded their array of community kitchens, others emphasized neighbourhood food gardens, while many relied on the distribution of food parcels. This diversity and emphasis on local needs form the nature of the movement and, I believe, a fascinating account of how platforms can enable decentralized community building. The model has spread to other parts of the country, but its origins in the Mother City and the density of its networks speak to structural qualities and spatial relationships that I return to in Chapter 6.

The proliferation of community gardens in some of the CAN neighbourhoods does shift the emphasis to the production part of the food chain. The climate crisis will continue to impact food security and having the data to understand the extent to which this is happening is an essential part of formulating resilience strategies. The final example in Chapter 4 highlights the use of drone technology to map the Zanzibar islands in Tanzania, a region that relies on agriculture as a dominant source of income. The mapping process is also seen as an act of empowerment for Muslim women, as they cross sociocultural boundaries to engage new technologies. The exclusionary dynamics that contribute to deepening urban poverty and marginalization are shown to be associated with political regimes and the inadequacies of governance. This theme recurs throughout the book and points to a tension between collective agency and governance frames. An angle of exploration is how new regimes are forged through techno-social relations in the political realm. Two of the vignettes discussed in Chapter 4 speak explicitly to the need to shift power dynamics and confront inequality. Understanding how social mobilization enables livelihoods and challenges state power is the subject of Chapter 5.

Digital platforms and social activism

The CAN initiative is representative of a form of community activism that is situated, informed by place and largely enabled through associational networks, both online and offline. The ability of city residents to challenge the state and corporate power is assisted by social media and community platforms, with the most prominent being WhatsApp. Popular protest appears to be both on the rise and simultaneously dispersed, showing a spectrum of social mobilization that, depending on and in response to different acts of the state, can range from formal, organized resistance to leaderless street politics, virtual defiance through social media and even acts of waiting. Digital platforms also have negative consequences, as shown in the impact of Airbnb on local property markets, as well as gentrification. The story of the Remain in the City campaign in Cape Town illustrates how disruption can be a two-sided coin, in that it can undermine housing access and unsettle livelihoods. Together with Ndifuna Ukwazi (NU), a social justice organization based in the city, this initiative succeeded in forcing the city of Cape Town to rethink its own stance on inclusionary housing. The focus of Chapter 5 is to develop the notion of cyborg activism as a form of mobilization that harnesses new technologies to expand networks, enabling a hybrid form of organizing that resists and resets power relations in the city.

I am interested in the diversity entailed in digitally enhanced livelihoods and the many entry points for disruption to make a difference through challenging governance from above and contributing to city management from below. However, oppositional practice is difficult in countries that have limited press freedom or curtail social mobilization. In some contexts, working more convivially with the state is more strategic. In Chapter 5, I explore how the power of data and generation of knowledge are critical to shifting views and policies on informal settlements in Sierra Leone. Of interest in relation to the theme of Chapter 5 is how analogue and digital resources are combined to form a flexible information and mobilization ecosystem. The SLURC in Freetown serves as an advocacy and co-productive research entity, particularly focused on enabling recognition of the urban informal economy. Working with affiliates of Shack/Slum Dwellers International (SDI) and its 'Know Your City' campaign, the centre uses online and offline tools to mobilize, collaborate and disseminate information, while providing a central focal point for digital data on the urban poor in the country.

In all of the foregoing, how data are represented and communicated is key to influencing policymakers. The use of video and infographics is combined with regular updates on WhatsApp and social media. I pay particular attention to how the suite of available platforms are combined and used to connect and inform, drawing on the work of NU and CTT primarily. In Chapter 5, the notion of experiential knowledge, that is, a qualitative engagement with the problems of the 'everyday', features in the work of such social movements as NU and CTT, as well as the patient labour of the SLURC. I also refer briefly to the use of drone photography in this regard. The notion of cyborg activism assists conceptually in making sense of how this may differ from past forms of engagement. I am clearly inspired by Donna Haraway in this regard, particularly her reference to the notion of 'world-changing fiction' in the following quotation: 'A cyborg is a cybernetic organism, a hybrid of machine and organism, a creature of social reality as well as a creature of fiction. Social reality is lived social relations, our most important political construction, a world-changing fiction' (Haraway, 1991: 149). An exploration of 'fictions' employed in social mobilization is one of the threads in Chapter 5 and is also explored in the conclusion of this book. However, a core part of storytelling is imagination and the aim to capture the public imagination in advancing a particular cause. Exploring cultural practices is essential to employing a postcolonial STS lens – an examination of the textures of technology appropriation as it relates to place.

Cultural practices and place making

What emerges from Chapters 3 to 5 is the hybrid nature of the disrupted city, where the 'old' and 'new' reinforce each other in an ongoing dance of socio-technical evolution, and how the ongoing rhythms of African urban spaces speak to global connections and local cultures (Ling and Horst, 2011).

In many ways, Chapter 6 explores the many imaginations of the digital city. It does this from three vantage points. The first explores intentional digital places that seek to use technology to define and articulate its textures (MapKibera) and establish global connections (iHubs). The second focuses on cultural practices. The entry point is an examination of the GoDown arts centre in Nairobi as a physical and digital melting pot of cultural talents, intended to disrupt urban space through cultural networking. The third dimension explores the cultural practices and representation of African urban futures through an examination of Afrofuturism as emblematic of the disrupted hybrid city. It is also the means whereby the future of society and technology are imagined. The aim in Chapter 6 is to look towards the future of African urban spaces by examining the present and how it engages the past.

The thread throughout this final thematic chapter is to not only follow on from the ambitions expressed in much of the social mobilization that I engaged in Chapter 5, but also look towards the future. Science fiction literature, cinema and popular explorations of the role of the digital in our everyday lives are profoundly informed by Northern constructs of the 21st-century citizen: urbane, generally North American or European, moneyed, and often male. The combination of the endogenous urban narratives, imagined technology-mediated futures and visual imagery that are captured in Chapter 6 unsettles these popular constructs. This provocation is a fitting entry point to my final conclusions on disruptive practices in African cities.

Finally

Threads or motifs that recur throughout the discussion of these vignettes inform the conclusion of the book on the socio-technical evolution of African cities. Data on these vignettes have been gathered through personal interviews, the perusal of online forums and social media, and reference to secondary and grey literature on these examples. To make sense of these examples, I frame this book in accordance with the aforementioned four substantive themes to answer a very straightforward question: if corporate smart promises are inadequate in responding meaningfully to urban challenges in Africa, how do disruptive practices that use digital platforms do so more effectively? This is the focus of the Chapter 7.

There is, of course, a theoretical aspiration also. The conceptual story is about how we make sense of socio-technical change in geographies that are politically unstable, spatially fragmented and highly inequitable. In Chapter 7, I am interested in how a postcolonial STS approach can enable the theoretical tools to continue such work into the future. The conceptual project underpinning this book is to destabilize and, to some extent, disrupt how we view technology and cities in Africa. My conclusions focus on the emerging qualities of this relationship: the importance of flow and connection in socio-technical relations; the centrality of trust and continuity in enabling the application of technology; the tensions between existing governance frames and emerging regimes as a result of digital evolution; and the African city as hybrid, that is, a messy entanglement of the old and the new.

Chapter 2 serves as a grounding in contemporary debates on digital platforms and cities. Towards this aim, I explore literature on platform urbanism in relation to contemporary socio-technical change in African cities. Nascent literature on 'platform urbanism' raises important questions about inequality and unevenness in the distribution of opportunities and benefits. In Chapter 2, platform urbanism is seen as a co-constitution of platform structures and urban space through a deepening of the geospatial dimensions of the platform economy (Stehlin et al, 2020). Söderström and Mermet (2020: 2) refer to one of the distinguishing features of platform urbanism as constituting 'modes of engagement with technology in urban everyday life', where the relationship between individuals and digital platforms has socio-spatial consequences. Impacts on the daily lives and governance of cities is questioned, as disruption typically precedes and outpaces regulation.

Typically, the features of platform urbanism cut across north–south boundaries through processes of formalization and informalization, sometimes through the same platforms (Stehlin et al, 2020). The relationship between disruption and city governance is therefore key to taking the debate on platform urbanism further, and this book seeks to contribute to that. While some work has been done on technology hubs and very specific features of the gig economy in African cities (Jiménez and Zheng, 2021), as well as its limitations (Friederici, 2018), what is largely missing from the more general literature on smart cities in the Global South, as well as the more recent work on platform urbanism, is an interrogation of the co-production of urban space through bottom-up innovation and disruption. Thus, as a theoretical project, this book builds on recent work on some of the relational trends in urban thinking, incorporating postcolonial STS, in arguing for a conceptual lens that operationalizes the notion of studying the city as a socio-technical construct, rather than the sum of its material and human parts.

2

The Expansive Nature of Platforms

Introduction

Some of the most nuanced and convincing work on digital communities is inspired by stories that enable learning and reflection. In many ways, this distinguishes between the fantasy imagery that informs the smart city visual narratives and the 'real' cities referred to in Chapter 1. The quantitative work on the application of smart technologies, the statistics on the range of uses and landscapes of digital access do, however, provide an important backdrop to the tales that unfold in urban settings. Contextualized accounts of the use of digital tools inform an instinctive yet rigorous socio-technical lens that sees human and material agency as co-productive. The ways through which new technologies are appropriated determine how they 'land' in particular contexts. That is not the end of the process, however; how they land and what contributes to the evolution of disruptive practices is intimately tied to the qualities of place (Aurigi and Odendaal, 2021). There is also a temporal dimension where, for example, digitally enabled problem solving 'on the go' in informal settings could change from day to day. Those living in particularly marginal circumstances use a 'suite' of tools at different times to negotiate city life. The aim of this chapter is to explore the conceptual lenses that enable such strategies to be surfaced.

A more finely grained approach to accounts of technology use is often contrary to the visual and technical narratives that portray the smart city. These often contrast with the textures of contemporary urban spaces. In Chapter 1, I outlined some of the issues that emerge when applying the smart city concept to African cities. Elsewhere, I have argued that the examination of socio-technical practices represents an opportunity for engaging contemporary urbanity in the Global South, as marginal circumstances often drive innovation through necessity (Odendaal, 2020). By exploring how technology and livelihoods rub up against each other, I answer the call of Söderström and McFarlane (among others) for an enquiry into 'how digital technologies might practically become embedded in the already existing worlds of urban life' (McFarlane and Söderström, 2017: 313). By offering a livelihood-centred view, technology appropriation is analysed as the driving force of smart urbanism, rather than the outcome of material elements and their algorithmic interpretations.

The literature on smart cities has expanded tremendously since the early days when William Mitchell (1996) observed workers 'pulling glass' outside his Cambridge, Massachusetts, home and Stephen Graham and Simon Marvin (1996) explored the spatial patterns of telecommunications in European cities. Early work on communities and technologies explored the social networking possibilities of the Internet (Haythornthwaite, 2005; Foth, 2006), with the notion of 'virtual capital' a significant feature of this work (Wellman et al, 2001). Later, the term 'urban informatics' took a more integrated view, seeing technology and urban life as co-evolutionary and co-constitutive (Foth, 2008; Shin, 2009). Thus, the work on technology and cities has generally spread itself across a number of disciplines, ranging from urban sociology to STS. In the Global South, the ICT for development (ICT4D) literature offers an important emphasis on the relationship between the state and technology. Early literature on e-governance highlighted some of the operational limitations of such in the Global South and its developmental prospects (Heeks, 2001; Madon, 2004; Madon et al, 2010). More recent work provides a critical engagement with the limitations of the state or, more poignantly, how technology is deployed to address the inadequacies of the state. In India, the apparent transparency enabled through e-governance, that is, the accountability enabled through digitally enhanced information sharing in real time, raises questions about ethics and citizenship (Datta, 2018). Datta's (2018) work on 'futuring' as a core state strategy in selling the smart city fantasy also looks to the past in providing insights into how that vision of the future is embedded in deepening the discursive relationship between nationhood and technology, as well as its connections to the past. The neoliberal goal of 'minimum government, maximum governance' does, indeed, raise concerns about corporate control of state governance (Datta, 2018). What Datta finds in her research is the ever-present gap between the totalizing discourse and the uncertainties and confusion on the ground in response to government-led smart strategies.

When examining the role of smart applications in everyday city life, the conceptual challenge is to open a space for research that scratches hard enough to reveal the inconsistencies, contradictions and frustrations embedded in practice. Not only are smart city ideas enrolled into policy discourses, but the boundaries between smart technologies and other service infrastructures are blurring, allowing for a broader array of actors to enter the city governance space. Implementation of digitally enhanced service delivery is not simply a matter of throwing technology at a problem, however. The broadening of the range of actors that now form part of the city governance arena, ranging from IBM to civil society organizations (CSOs), implies a deepening of power dynamics related to private capital and public policy. I have argued elsewhere that the increasing proliferation of digital platforms, for example, has led to a more distributed agency that not only refers to the financial reach of such firms as Airbnb and Uber, but also creates opportunities for endogenous digital initiatives, some of which are used to challenge the urban inequalities entrenched through platform urbanism (Odendaal, 2022) a point I explore in more detail later. The use of digital tools for social activism provides many opportunities for expression and mobilization (Cardullo, 2020; Gerbaudo, 2012). Together with the usual offline mechanics of activism, online media available for information dissemination and publicity has been well harnessed towards social justice in, for example, South African cities (Mitchell and Odendaal, 2015), with data having been reconceptualized as a tool of storytelling towards social activism (Odendaal, 2019). Social media enables connection and dissemination, often underpinning dissension practices that are 'living indicators' (Kaika, 2017) of urban life at the margins, with smart solutions and innovation embedded in these dissention practices. Cardullo (2020: 109) refers to an 'incipient municipalism', where cities are challenging the neoliberal manifestations of the platform economy and embracing what he terms 'an alternative version of smartness' that puts citizens' needs first.

No doubt, civil society activity will intensify as urban challenges deepen, but such uses are not necessarily confrontational. The corporate landscape of telecommunications provides opportunities for a diversity of small-scale actors to become part of the ICT market and beyond. These range from pop-up community-based projects that utilize technology towards cultural expression to crowd-sourced digital mapping in what Cardullo (2020: 81) refers to as 'living labs'. Many of these take on heterogeneous configurations that include analogue as well as digital applications. For example, the celebrated MapKibera project in Nairobi, Kenya, combines online mapping of landmarks within Kibera informal settlements with community radio and physical renderings on public walls to enable spatial legibility and public safety (Odendaal, 2018). Unravelling these assemblages of tech, community action and physical expression within their place-based contexts provides a useful reminder of the contingency of technology innovation. Some of this may find expression in the mobilization tactics of social movements, or in the day-to-day problem solving of urban dwellers. Increasingly, this is finding expression in the urban infrastructure realm, as smart applications are becoming increasingly common in the provision and maintenance of city utilities. This allows for a range of actors and agencies to collaborate in providing infrastructure. Guma's work in Nairobi examines the spatial, social and political dynamics of such assemblages. Approaching Nairobi (the Silicon Savannah) as a testbed for innovation, Guma (2019) uncovers the political contingencies and contestations that emerge from the use of ICT tools in mediating water and electricity supply. This is significant, in that it draws on Simone's (2004) notion of 'people as infrastructure' in uncovering the intricacies of infrastructure constellations. In particular, he shows how residents recalibrate and repurpose technology inputs into service provision to serve their needs. This is not a straightforward story of empowerment and addressing inequality. Much like I found in my study of ICT distribution in Durban, South Africa, access patterns tend to echo private investment strategies, not the public goals of equitable access (Odendaal, 2011). While references to smart cities might celebrate large-scale innovation and technical solutions to intractable spatial problems, infrastructure-led approaches seldom deliver on some of the more grandiose promises of what Graham and Marvin (2001) refer to as the 'modern infrastructure ideal' of evenly distributed access.

The literature on smart cities and urbanism provides an important backdrop to considering the appropriation role of technology in contemporary urbanism. Themes that emerge include innovation, governance, infrastructure assemblage and activism, which will recur as leitmotifs that permeate the stories contained in this book. What is important for the aims of this book, however, is the consideration of the agency dynamics at the interface of the technical and human. The more recent literature on platforms and cities provides a more immediate and contemporary literature base for such insights. It also provides the point of departure from which I develop my conceptual position taken in the analysis of this material: an elaboration on the postcolonial STS literature. The recent emphasis on platforms creates an opportunity for a more robust formulation of postcolonial STS given how digital platforms are so entrenched in the 'everyday'.

Smart versus platform urbanism

As a term, 'smart urbanism' evolved from 'smart cities' and describes, and analyses, how smart technologies and infrastructures are integrated into everyday life. Willis and Aurigi's (2017) distinction in the use of the terms is useful: whereas the smart city is often considered as a stand-alone entity that incorporates the technologies enabling the functioning of the city and its administration, smart urbanism considers how the material, economic and social are enrolled into its continued unfolding. Thinking about how technology influences urban life on an ongoing basis, 'the city comes to be known through data, algorithms, modelling and a combination of visual and media channels' (Willis and Aurigi, 2017: 42), as well as new ways of understanding and imagining the city (Marvin et al, 2015). Marvin and Luque-Ayala (2017) refer to 'urban operating systems' as routines whereby big data and the IoT are combined with city management processes in governance. The debates have evolved with technology innovation as researchers make sense of the interface between city functioning and infrastructure evolutions.

Much of the smart urbanism literature is situated in the Global North, with its attendant circumstances, assuming ubiquitous access to technology, strong government and good backbone infrastructure. In the Global South, as outlined in the introduction, smart urbanism tends to be equated with developmental objectives. More recent STS-informed analyses and some in the political-ecology literature emphasize heterogeneity, but they are rare and tend to focus more broadly on urban services (Furlong, 2010, 2014; Lawhon et al, 2014). I believe that thinking about digital platforms in relation to urban life, or what is referred to as 'platform urbanism', is a more contemporary and relevant point of departure for thinking about digital disruption in African cities.

While the term 'platform' was used as early as the 1990s, it was with the development of Web 2.0 that the value of reciprocity became apparent in the relationship between consumer and producer. Connectivity and integration are now core functions of the technical infrastructure, allowing for data exchange with developers of complimentary applications. The proliferation of platforms expands the myriad of actors that now play in the city space, mediating many areas of life. Some argue that the platform economy represents a hegemonic commercial frame that is based on the capacity of multinational firms to extract value from the connectivity enabled through technology and the networks that emanate from that, rather than through investment in labour and production (Stehlin et al, 2020). It also shapes the practices of participants, thereby embedding the power of the platform economy (Sadowski, 2020b). The materiality of software platforms is often hard to discern, but their impacts are becoming more obvious. Wiig and Masucci (2020), as well as Guma and Monstadt (2020), show a relationship between the operations of platforms and urban inequalities, with gentrification impacts recorded in many cities (Cocola-Gant and Gago, 2019). The impact on land markets and, by extension, housing and service access has been the focus of much urban activism, from Barcelona (Wilson et al, 2020) to Cape Town (Odendaal, 2021a, 2021b). Thus, there are a range of explorations of how the platform economy manifests in cities, with an overriding thematic exploration of the power of technology capital as a force to be weary of. In one of the first systematic accounts of platform urbanism, Sarah Barns' more hopeful view suggests that the user is not a passive victim of corporate power; rather, agency emerges from the socio-technical assemblages that get formed in the use of platform infrastructure: 'Engaging with platform services is today an integral part of being an urban citizen and as such involves many different kinds of value-sharing, not only the value extracted by technology companies' (Barns, 2019: 576).

The play between corporate power, as expressed in the proliferation of digital platforms, and the agency afforded to users, or, more specifically, consumers, reveals a dynamic worthy of some discussion and contributes to the conceptual base of this book. What comes through in the literature is the tension between profit seeking and developer expression. Consideration of the architecture of digital platforms is an important premise for unveiling the possibilities for an expanded view on agency in this regard.

Digital platforms enable functional connections between a range of inputs. These inputs from application developers allow the platform's reach and functionality to expand within tightly controlled software parameters. The application programming interface (API) is the key enabler of software overlay and interaction. Hosted by the platform, it is an important piece of infrastructure that connects the functionality of the host platform to contributors and participants. The expansion of platform functionality is part of its business model, with strict protocols and rules that are framed by the platform host. Agency is informed by the ability to act, or, in this context, to develop and expand on the platform's functionality: 'digital remixing practices alter the traditional boundary between producers and consumers of cultural content' (Plantin et al, 2016: 6). Distinguishing between producers and consumers of cultural content, and the blurring of the traditional boundary between them, is what creates a space for the consideration of agency more carefully.

The dual agency of platforms is thus innovation and expansion, on the one hand, and constrained participation in accordance with the platform business model, on the other. Agency is determined by the extent to which users can go beyond the platform intentions and influence its programmability. How much the API is exposed is determined by how finely the platform host seeks to integrate other applications. Exposure of functionality is controlled by a 'key' issued by the platform in accordance with the parameters that inform coding practices and interface requirements. Expansion of platform functionality is enabled through carefully formulated frames and rules. In some ways, an open-ended but contingent agency is performed in the relationship that requires negotiation in relation to platform API exposure.

Agency is expressed in communication, expansion of the functionality of the platform and knowledge production. Opportunities for innovation and expansion are enabled through varying degrees of control. Three components shape the infrastructure of platforms: the core, which has low variability; the complimentary systems, with high variability; and the interfaces for modularity between these two (Plantin et al, 2016). The agility of the interface between the core and complimentary applications allows opportunities for innovation because the whole system does not need to be reformed when new innovations are added. The parameters determined by the core ensure that the system is stable.

Data are the currency that determine the levels of exposure allowed by the API. How data are collected, re-represented and reorganized is informed by platform profit objectives. The protection of personal data is, of course, very important and is becoming a dominant public debate as governments intervene through the regulation of social media platforms. Data storage and app generation are determined by API rules (Pink et al, 2020) and determine knowledge production capacity. Making data available for public applications, such as municipal open data portals, or local government hackathons that foster programming capacity have become vehicles through which 'smartness' can be more evenly distributed. Knowledge expansion is enabled through the combination of the data processing capacity of digital technologies and skills developed in the deployment of these applications. These data are embedded at different scales: in smart devices, in concentrator or 'fog' devices (such as routers), in embedded servers, in video surveillance cameras, and in cloud servers (Pink et al, 2020). Fog computing forms the interface between the production of data and cloud storage, with open data advocates stressing the need for opening this space through sharing the knowledge and expertise more generally in the public interest. Examples where digital data and technology deployment are driven by citizens are weather and air quality applications, or such publicly developed kits as the Air Quality Egg and Smart Citizen Kit discussed by Pink, Ardèvol and Lanzeni (2020). The authors discuss the potential for an 'ethnographic place' (Pink, 2009), where 'different types, qualities and temporalities of things and persons come together as part of the process of the making of ethnographic knowledge' (Pink and Morgan, 2013: 354). Spaces of heterogeneous knowledge production are made possible through design, technology and human encounters. As Pink (2016) finds in her ethnographic work on citizen-centred applications: 'They undertook their own knowledge-based processes in this "place", shaping in that encounter what material means to them, and bringing into existence possible technologies that they imagined, based on their experiential knowledge from other projects' (Pink et al, 2020: 60). Such factors impact the relationships between digital media, technologies and people, as well as the diverse forms of media and what aspects of our lives they influence. Expanding the operations of platforms into the public sphere has implications for urban infrastructure. As Plantin et al (2016: 3) claim: 'Digital technologies have made possible a "platformization" of infrastructure and an "infrastructuralization" of platforms.'

The power and currency of software contribute to the functioning of infrastructure space. Whether through smart grids or the deployment of domestic water meters, digital applications enable the central monitoring of use and citizen-based monitoring. In their exploration of the functional qualities of platforms in relation to urban infrastructure, Plantin et al (2016: 5) highlight one of the key systemic differences: 'platform builders do not seek to internalize their environments through vertical integration. Instead, their platforms are designed to be extended and elaborated from outside, by other actors, provided that those actors follow certain rules.' I would argue that this could be a source of tension when considering the differences between platform and urban infrastructure governance systems. Part of what 'locks in' urban infrastructure functioning, such as energy supply or water reticulation, are professional regimes that include the norms and standards governing operations. Expansion or a change in the system have not only material implications, but also knock-on effects on maintenance and governance. In the Global South, many of the engineering regimes and urban planning codes that govern infrastructure delivery and maintenance are inherited from colonial institutions and, in many cases, are still in use and stubbornly obdurate. Many follow funding guidelines of aid or bilateral organizations. Outdated or inappropriate implementation standards become problematic in informal settings or in resource-scarce environments where infrastructure expansion is fiscally impossible. A worthy exploration would be to examine how technology disruption that interfaces with urban infrastructure may overcome some of these limitations.

Informality is a feature of housing and employment in African cities, as discussed in Chapter 1. Confronting infrastructure backlogs and livelihoods would require an imagination that sees the formal–informal spectrum as an essential part of African urbanity, and this impacts infrastructure governance systems but could be assimilated into platforms. An example is SafeBoda, an app developed in Uganda for motorcycle taxis, discussed in Chapter 3. Essentially an 'informal' form of public transport, the *boda-boda* industry is continuously subject to official scrutiny due to high accident figures, road safety concerns and general issues regarding safe transportation. The construction of a digital platform for *boda-boda* riders represents an intriguing interface between the adjustable API of the platform and the *boda-boda* culture and its own forms of organization. This assemblage, consisting of the SafeBoda platform, its operatives, its drivers and city infrastructure, has since been expanded to include street vendors that produce food, as well as medical supplies during COVID-19. The platform has also been exported to other cities. As explored in Chapter 3, there is opportunity for insurgency and improved livelihoods, but literature from elsewhere shows that it does impact on materiality, daily lives and the governance of cities (Söderström and Memet, 2020). Worthy of exploration is the extent to which the platform scaffolding allows for a limited formalization of practices within a governance frame that illegitimates them. What the digital platform ostensibly represents is a seemingly pliable frame for multi-actor collaboration and, at its most hopeful, innovation.

As discussed earlier, the platform is a producer and conveyor of data. The flow and production of information impact on how the material elements of infrastructure are organized (Easterling, 2014). The agency that emerges from platform assemblages is contingent, despite their 'multiple layered invisibilities' (Furlong, 2020: 7). This does not just refer to large-scale technical systems, redesigned and adapted to enable digital monitoring and customer feedback loops, such as smart grids and decentralized water metering systems. There are implications from examining endogenous platforms in African cities for how infrastructure providers adopt platform systems and protocols. Also of interest are lower-cost, sometimes more contextually appropriate, urban infrastructure solutions that are more attuned to livelihoods, such as smart meters in informal areas (Baptista, 2015) and in Cape Town (Jaglin, 2008). The agile nature of the platform has opened up scope for diversity and non-capitalist experimentation through heterogeneous practices across scales and social structures (Stehlin et al, 2020). However, as shown by Guma (2020) in Nairobi, these platforms are often associated with private enterprises, ignorant of local needs and networks. In many ways, the platform literature needs to mature to the extent that the public interest is considered in the ways that we think through the human elements of infrastructure: practices, habits, organizational culture and structural impacts.

The expansion of platforms to include everyday practices potentially leads to atomized access that can, in fact, perpetuate inequality. It also opens up 'opportunities' for hacking, sometimes through nefarious and potentially dangerous practices, such as illegal electricity connections and/or meter tampering. The impacts of such practices are material of course, often enabling broadened service access but with damaging effects to meters for example. These arrangements also result in networks of actors that include cartels, community groups, private service providers and policing groups (Guma, 2020). They speak of a contemporary urbanism that appropriates the technological enablers of infrastructure provision in accordance with the rules determined by context and place.

Space, agency and platforms

Urban policymakers and planners have long given up the notion that they are the sole creators of urban places. The addition of platform urbanism to this dynamic is that the range of actors contributing to the distribution of infrastructure has broadened, and this has spatial implications that result in forms of place making that may look quite different from that in planning manuals. The impact of platforms on space is more diverse and variable, being subject to local markets and heterogeneous practices, as APIs allow for reinterpretation of urban issues and solutions. These practices can travel, thanks to the platform, yet can find their unique calibrations when they land in particular places (Pollio, 2019). Local interpretations are subject to regulations (Firmino et al, 2019), local political-economy ambitions and city visioning (Pollio, 2019), as well as survival networks (Guma, 2020). However, they are also subject to local legacies of spatial inequalities, as shown in Philadelphia (Wiig and Masucci, 2020) and Cape Town (Odendaal, 2019). Urban platforms co-constitute the city; in fact, there is a co-generative dynamic between digital platforms and urban life (Barns, 2019), though in a finely grained manner, as the dynamics of the 'everyday' are enrolled into the functionality of platforms (Söderström and Mermet, 2020).

The intersection between platform and infrastructure studies suggests a spatial configuration that is potentially driven by more distributed agency, departing from the path-breaking notion of urban splintering posited by Graham and Marvin (2001). When considering the evolution of infrastructure studies (Plantin et al, 2016), the latest iteration of webs of infrastructure, rather than networks, does imply spatial forms that are not splintered, but perhaps more differentiated and dynamic in urban form. The agility of the platform, in that it can enrol new actors quickly and sidestep regulation, means that changes on the ground could potentially change quickly also. In many ways, it implies instability. Mark Graham's (2020) notion of 'conjectural geographies' is relevant here. The speculative nature of platform urbanism does mean that firms can not only link themselves to local contexts to optimize reward, but also retreat to the regulatory regimes of host countries when challenged, in what Graham (2020: 454) refers to as their 'ephemeral digital dualisms'.

Interrogating the influence of platforms does therefore require 'multiple epistemological strategies for the interpretation of urban life, in ways that recognise diverse sites of socio-spatial encounter, beyond ontologies of control, transaction and appropriation' (Barns, 2019: 9). Graham (2020) posits three ways through which alternative platform futures can be created or existing dynamics can be subverted: regulation, replication and/or resistance. Through home-grown mobility apps, cooperative alternatives to Airbnb or subverted use possibilities for a range of urban practices that could offer more hope for urban dwellers are on the rise. Whether it could lead to an overall spatial form that is more accessible and equitable remains to be seen. It could, indeed, lead to pockets of inclusion and exclusion, as assemblages of infrastructure actors coalesce in some areas at the expense of others, or it could, indeed, simply accelerate trends of exclusion, such as seen in the property market in Cape Town (Odendaal, 2019), or perpetuate the spatial mismatch between employment and skills among people living in post-industrial spaces (Wiig and Masucci, 2020). We may see urban forms that display more atomic clustering, being temporally unstable and dependent on digital connection and platform enrolment, in what Stehlin et al (2020: 15) refer to as 'an uneven geography of saturation in some places and exclusion in others – both within and across cities'. Platforms target individuals, but they also connect and enable interaction, hence the need to re-examine the notion of agency in relation to urban spaces.

As discussed earlier, the platform API provides the interface between platform owner and developer, acting in a 'recombinatory' way (Barns, 2019), decentralizing the creation of value-added yet centralizing data collection and value capture. This intermediary function of platforms enables a diversity of inputs and a range of choices for the consumer (or 'partner'), and speaks to the performative power of platforms and their associated algorithms. Nevertheless, this is a set of relations that constantly needs to be performed and negotiated, allowing for expression within a corporate frame. Stehlin et al (2020) refer to three ways through which urban space and platforms can intersect more meaningfully: the redistributive potential of platforms; favourable intersections with urban life; and impacting the interface with socio-spatial inequalities. Research in Kenya (Guma, 2020; Odendaal 2020) shows that this is not necessarily a static situation, for example, start-ups may start with donor funding and then evolve into fully fledged enterprises. The objectives of such initiatives may change over time, resulting in changing spatial impacts. Temporal dimensions are important. Networked infrastructure regimes are obdurate and take a long time to change. Platforms are guided by internal protocols but are nevertheless more short term in their impact as inputs evolve and changes to applications are made. The lack of regulation, of course, deepens this dynamic where regulations do not keep up with disruption. What this implies is that the impacts of platforms can be enacted in a fairly short period but could have long-term impacts.

Whereas networked infrastructure regimes are subject to the aforementioned professional norms, government regulations and standards, the individualized nature of platforms frustrates efforts at governance. Yet, it also allows for problem solving when substantive issues are not dealt with, such as mobility in Kenya and Uganda (Odendaal, 2020), access to safe mobility and job creation in South Africa (Pollio, 2019), and the ability for households to budget incrementally for electricity in Mozambique (Baptista, 2015). Data power informs the relationship between vendors and individuals, which, in turn, influences and permeates urban life. What emerges is a distributed agency that may result in spatial expressions led through cooperatives, citizen groups or corporations. Whereas data and financial power are vested with platform owners, a reordering of agency interests potentially emerges from the other side of the API, leading to rapid change and deployment, astute problem solving, and social mobilization. Social media, for example, does allow for a broader range of voices and technical and cultural environments, as well as a reordering of meaning and information (Rodgers and Moore, 2020). Not only that, but emerging from such spaces is also a platform for urban storytelling that serves as a counter to centralized data-driven discourses (Odendaal, 2019). Rodgers and Moore (2020: 220) refer to algorithms as possessing 'secondary agency', where online political actions are part of situated practices and material spaces. Social practices and mobilization are issue driven and will find their platform spaces when and where appropriate.

Two notions appear to emerge when considering the interrelationship between cities and platforms: the notion of a web (rather than a network) of infrastructure configurations that can be quite disconnected from one another, completely debunking the notion of the 'modernist infrastructure ideal' (Graham and Marvin, 2001) of ubiquitous services provision; and the 'hub and spoke' notion, as platform APIs enrol developers and content providers in their operations. What 'messes' with these two figurative notions is the idea of 'place' and everything that it represents: history, governance, environmental quality, citizenship and so on. Whereas in urban planning terms, the notion of place is intertwined with the qualitative characteristics of physical spaces, I refer here to a broader interpretation that recognizes these more 'invisible' features as ongoing inputs into how platforms land in African cities. This has been explored in infrastructure studies, political ecology (Lawhon et al, 2014), urban studies (Baptista, 2015) and work on smart urbanism by Guma (2020) and Odendaal (2020). This work recognizes diversity in infrastructure assemblages, while also acknowledging the distributed nature of agency.

Multidirectional agency and science and technology studies

Spatial constraints do not simply disappear with broadened technology access; rather, they coexist with cyberspace in a hybrid form (Graham, 2008) that is more relational than Cartesian (Odendaal, 2014). Some *places* remain isolated and under-serviced; what new technologies offer is access to digitally connected *spaces*. This is the hopeful and now slightly outdated version of the claims of ICT4D and smart urbanism: the notion that technology enables inclusion through functional association. COVID-19 has come to highlight the limited digital connection that many experience due to spatial isolation or poverty, and how this impacts survival. Recent literature indicates that the platform economy mimics the spatial impacts of post-industrial spatial policies (Wiig and Masucci, 2020) and exclusionary macroeconomic trends (Pollio, 2019). In short, the presence of technology is not enough. In addition to infrastructure investment, technology access is mediated through livelihood strategies and individual appropriation, particularly in marginal socio-economic circumstances (Odendaal, 2011; Guma, 2019). To return to the notion of capturing stories referred to at the beginning of this chapter, uncovering these instances of urbanity where technology is enrolled into the everyday is a means to gain insight into moments of empowerment.

Uncovering how these processes can be tweaked, what opportunities they present for more inclusive cities and what they mean for livelihoods in general, thereby provincializing the study of digital and associated infrastructure, makes sense. The term 'provincialization' refers to focusing the analytical lens on the histories, geographies and political economies of the postcolonial, where global ideas land, are reinterpreted and are reinvented. Thus, this postcolonial term is not about rejecting Western/Northern debates or only embracing Eastern/Southern experiences (Chakrabarty et al, 2007); rather, it opens analyses to how a phenomenon is tied to, and generated by, place, with a broader range of urban experiences. It is a sensibility, or, what Lawhon, Ernstson and Silver (2014: 505) describe as, 'an epistemological location, rather than a geographical container'. Hence, literature informed by STS, as well as work on African urbanism, guide the reflection of the vignettes contained in this book.

STS enables a socio-technical gaze that allows for infrastructure to be considered in relation to its geographic, institutional and political context. These social studies of scientific knowledge are essentially focused on how the sciences and their locations co-produce and co-constitute each other (Harding, 2009). They embrace change as socio-technical, driven as much by human agency as by scientific innovation. Postcolonialism requires a decentring of the subject and a rejection of the modernist notion that scientific rationality and technical expertise will somehow enable progress, despite being disengaged from local knowledge systems. Postcolonial STS more specifically rejects the notion of scientific knowledge as inherently Western and rational, and challenges Western philosophies of science and conventional epistemologies. It emerges from a critique of science studies in relation to the South, where standard accounts of the history of science are examined and where the location of modern scientific thought in relation to context is questioned. Some of this work has found its way into other disciplines, but its application to the roles played by digital tools in developing countries is rare. Published work on utility infrastructure and the battles to gain access to essential services in very marginal circumstances, for example, in informal settlements, provides valuable insights in this regard. In their formulation of the notion of 'heterogeneous infrastructure configurations', Lawhon et al (2018) draw mainly from African cases in their discussions, showing how the material elements of infrastructural systems relate to socio-technical configurations embedded with risks and power relations. Heterogeneity refers to a spectrum of material artefacts, uses and users enrolled into a dynamic configuration (Lawhon et al, 2018). These deep contextual accounts of continued methods of repair, assembly and creation lead to incremental changes that could potentially be emancipatory (Summerton, 1994, cited in Lawhon et al, 2018).

There are two concepts that surface that are well worth exploring as informants to the explorations in this book. The analytical symmetry afforded to human and material agency is significant. Affording equal attention to the human and non-human in socio-technical networks is a standard relational trick, informed by actor–network theory (ANT). The focus is not so much on the individual technical elements, but on the collective agency that emerges from use. Here, the notion of assemblage explored more recently in urban studies (Anderson and McFarlane, 2011; Farías and Bender, 2012) is useful, as it emphasizes the heterogeneous qualities of networks of human and non-human actors as 'a multiplicity of processes of becoming, affixing sociotechnical networks, hybrid collectives and alternative topologies' (Farias and Bender, 2012: 2). The open-ended nature of heterogeneous relations speaks to the notion of emergence and contingency (Anderson and McFarlane, 2011: 124). Rather than a grand theory, assemblage thinking represents an approach, that is, a lens that allows for both the material and the nascent and dynamic properties of relations to surface. It allows for analysis which recognizes that agency can emerge in unexpected places.

There are two entry points for a discussion on assemblage when considering the themes of this book: one is the consideration of connections between human and non-human actors in the ongoing negotiation of access to the city; the second relates to learning and innovation. The notion of assemblage as a verb, that is, as a descriptor of a process, rather than an outcome, leaves conceptual space for uncovering relations that are becoming in the process of establishing rules and parameters, which is a feature of urban life. The emphasis on the open-ended nature of assemblage focuses attention on the contingency and temporality of relations across space: 'assemblage connotes emergence rather than resultant formation' (Anderson and McFarlane, 2011: 125). This is useful when thinking of the emerging nature of platforms and the lack of institutional infrastructure to regulate and enable them. Recent work on drone technologies in East Africa, for example, shows a tandem process whereby the use of drones for humanitarian assistance co-evolves with negotiations around legal frameworks for their use (Lockhart et al, 2021). Innovative applications of these tools often precede the legal frameworks necessary to govern them.

The architecture of digital platforms enables software engineers and users to expand on platform applications within a set of user interface rules and data protocols. Platforms consist of material, digital and human elements, being constellations of code, developers, users and data. Elsewhere, I have argued that these constellations possess a multidirectional agency (Odendaal, 2022). How digital platforms or any smart applications 'land' in particular places is determined as much by their embedded encoding and software rules as by how they are put to work in particular contexts. These emerging assemblages or configurations are shaped by global technologies and local practices. Warwick Andersen (2002: 652) describes them as 'contact zones': 'simultaneously sites of multivocality; of negotiation, borrowing, and exchange; and of redeployment and reversal' – a situatedness that 'might offer us threads to follow through the labyrinth'. Postcolonial STS recognizes that even the longest networks are local at all points. Focusing on the '"situatedness" of "technoscience", as simultaneous sites of negation, borrowing and exchange' (Anderson, 2002: 651), enables a deeply contextual reading of the interface between human and material agency. Methodologically, it implies acceptance of contingency and flux. This entails an interrogation of the centre along with the periphery, accepting that the local is part of a series of connections through persons, practices and artefacts (Anderson, 2002: 652). The global and local are everywhere and articulated in accordance with the nature of practices and place.

What is less clear is how these practices, such as they are, contribute to problem solving in the local context, or, within the aims of this book, contribute to more workable cities that look nothing like their Northern counterparts yet provide solutions to intractable urban problems in contextually appropriate ways. One way through which such 'situatedness' can be probed in socio-technical relations is through understanding of the everyday practices of urbanites as they interface with infrastructure. A focus on everyday practices serves as a conceptual inversion and foregrounds people as infrastructure (Simone, 2004; Lawhon et al, 2014). Literature on Southern and African urbanism (Pieterse, 2014; Parnell and Pieterse, 2014) subverts the notion that cities in the South, or in Africa, are simply in the making, deficient in relation to an idealized notion of the optimal city. Understanding how cities dominated by informality and infrastructure backlogs truly function has practical implications. Developing an infrastructure that enables economic production demands an engagement with the relations that define trade and the exchange of goods and services. In the African context, these relations are perhaps less predictable where large numbers of people lack access to employment, social amenities and basic services. In many cases, livelihoods entail mobility: between cities, between the rural and urban, and often across borders (Simone, 2010). These circuits rarely coincide with the spatial delineations of conventional infrastructural networks.

The implications are twofold: first, existing service infrastructural potential is not maximized to effectively facilitate employment and economic growth; and, second, misguided infrastructure investments may constrain mobility and livelihoods – 'This is more than simply building new roads, rails, power lines, and telecommunications. It is more than a matter of constructing synergies between the physical, the institutional, the economic, and the informational' (Simone, 2010: 29). What this means for studies of digital disruption in African cities is the need to gain insight into how networks are constructed and maintained, and how that ties in with how technology is appropriated. What the more recent literature on STS suggests is that the situatedness of these milieus requires deeper understanding (Anderson, 2002; Philip et al, 2012) and that the heterogeneous assemblages that emerge in well-resourced spaces (Furlong, 2010), as well as in the cities of the Global South (Lawhon et al, 2018; Guma, 2019), show that human ingenuity, reinvention at the margins and continued appropriation require a lens that sees urban change as iterative and experimental. Philip, Irani and Dourish (2012) argue that the cultural dynamics of place are understudied in STS, while Furlong (2010) contends that as an approach, it tends to privilege the technical at the expense of the more nuanced dynamics of socio-political processes. The 'local' can be rendered quite abstract, devoid of geographic and temporal specificity (Philip et al, 2012). Engaging the everyday modalities of the appropriation of technology requires an engagement with messiness. Simone (2011) calls for a surfacing of what may undermine, change, alter or simply ignore notions of order and efficiency, not as responses to hardships, but as co-contributors to contemporary frames of urban life.

Spaces for learning and creativity can then be uncovered through recognition of the materiality of the digital and how that interfaces with the everyday. Micro-level 'socio-technical niches' encompass small networks of actors that add new technologies to the agenda, promoting innovations and novel technological developments. This may reveal configurations of actors hitherto unexplored in studies of technology and infrastructure transition. How social learning from niches can be applied at the city scale to help reshape the existing infrastructure regime is a challenge that requires a multi-scalar perspective that is mindful of the connections necessary for survival. The aim is to uncover not only the actors, institutions and infrastructures enabling beneficial change, but also the relations between them. It is through such relations that agencies emerge.

This, however, is not just a relational exercise, aimed at exploring livelihood strategies *in situ*. There are structural determinants of urban life that impact the everyday strategies of citizens. On the other hand, the 'pushing back' from the bottom up could very well be shifting the many conditions that determine city functioning. In the following four chapters, I select four sets of issues that I believe to be crucial to the future of African cities. In the discussion of each, I consider a selection of vignettes that illustrate digital appropriation in response to these thematic issues. The aim is to explore the extent to which the status quo can be unsettled through such practices. The first theme is an inquiry into mobility systems in Uganda and Kenya.

3

Hacking Mobility

Introduction

Kampala is not a particularly big city. In 2019, the population of the Ugandan capital was just under 1.5 million, with the metropolitan population estimated at 3.3 million.[1] Traversing the central city, however, can take the better part of two hours as *matatus* (the East African term for minivan taxis), four-by-four vehicles, sedans and motorcycle taxis compete for precious commuter space. *Boda-bodas* started as bicycle taxis in the 1960s in the Kenyan town of Busia, where they were used to smuggle goods across the border to Uganda, and have since retained their name (Mutiso and Behrens, 2011). The transformation of *boda-bodas* into informal 'for hire' transport services that range from passenger use to the running of errands and goods delivery has made this mode an essential part of Kampala's transportation system. As ubiquitous as *boda-bodas* are, however, they are very contested.

I first came across this antagonism when I was asked to speak on a panel on smart cities in Africa at an event at Makerere University in Kampala in November 2019. I shared the podium with an official from the Kampala City Capital Authority (KCCA) and the chief operations officer (COO) of SafeBoda, a Ugandan mobile platform for *boda-boda* riders. Proceedings got off to a rocky start when the KCCA official thinly disguised his dismissal of the *boda-boda* industry, arguing for limitations on numbers and strong-arm regulation. I was familiar with this sensibility. In the ten years that I have worked on the African continent, the unease and sometimes downright hostility towards the informal is depressingly familiar. The French term *transport artisanal* is perhaps more nuanced in acknowledging that these are demand-responsive systems: home-grown, deeply contextual and appropriate to local needs. The concept of 'artisanal transport' goes beyond stigmatizing paratransit (Godard, 2008: 1–2), allowing for it to be analysed in conjunction with more conventional modes. The relationship between the formal and informal is sometimes unclear, as it brings the topic of regulation into the equation. This appears to be the crux of the debate: how to enable effective regulation while allowing for demand to be met through less formal means. The addition of the IoT into the transport sector has muddied the waters somewhat and reveals many shades of regulatory grey when considering the range of options available in African cities. This is a running theme of this book: the ongoing dance between disruption and regulation. I shall return to this towards the end of this chapter as it relates to mobility and technology disruption.

As discussed in Chapter 2, the ubiquity of platform urbanism as an international phenomenon that has found its place in the Global South, and increasingly in African cities, represents a range of opportunities for local and multinational players in the mobility industry. The range of disruptions explored here include ride-hailing apps in Kenya and South Africa, as well as the SafeBoda experience that started in Uganda. I use this chapter to explore how these disruptions cannot be seen in substantive terms, but rather are deeply relational and give us clues as to how socio-technical changes in African cities may impact on city futures. Different styles of platform formation can, of course, result in uneven geographies of saturation, with the hope that publicly owned and cooperative platform mobilities possibly make a more even impact (Stehlin et al, 2020). The question, then, would be: are publicly owned platforms a possibility in urban contexts where institutions are weak and fiscal reach is very limited? The relational perspective adopted in this book, and discussed in Chapter 2, allows for differentiated and contextualized accounts of embedded disruption.

A consideration of the winners and losers in the 'shared economy' in contexts with high income inequality and structural legacies of socio-technical change begs an examination into the hidden costs of platform urbanism. In this chapter, I explore how such landings signal beginnings and are not corporate fait accomplis. In African countries, as in other parts of the Global South, the global impacts of the digital revolution have coincided, and, in some ways, contributed to, increased labour insecurity. In the Brazilian context, Firmino, Cardoso and Evangelista (2019: 206) refer to it as 'the blurring of the boundaries between work and non-work – a distinction that has been rendered meaningless by the computer, the internet, and the smartphone'. As in many parts of the Global North too, the precarious nature of work is revealed through the disruptions that Uber and other ride-hailing apps have caused in the urban sphere. Of immediate concern in the documented research on such ride-hailing apps as Uber, for example, is the layering of informal economic arrangements on exploitative (informal) practices under a gaze of surveillance technology. The assemblages that make up the platform economy in Global South contexts are deeply entangled with disjuncture and tensions between economic empowerment and exploitation, as the fluidity of such landings intersect with economic and labour histories, questioning the 'normative, "siliconvalleyan" rationalities' of technology firms (Pollio, 2019: 762).

While the focus on the exclusionary dynamics of the gig economy and platform urbanism is no doubt important, the point made that contextual differences produce very different experiences is an important one and does relate to the theoretical endeavour of this book: exploring the nuances of postcolonial STS. How platforms 'land' in difference contexts is informed by colonial histories, postcolonial interpretations and relations: 'In Brazil, we would say this is a move toward the tropicalization of global technologies, producing very specific ways in which these technologies are appropriated by local actors and resulting in unexpected situations' (Firmino et al, 2019: 207). This impacts the very fine line between exploitation and entrepreneurialism, as explored by Firmino et al (2019) in Brazil. In particular, they focus on the implicit function of the smartphone as a form of surveillance through real-time monitoring, for example, in their use of the term 'surveillance capitalism'. Pollio raises a similar point in his work on Uber in Cape Town, South Africa. While drivers see themselves as entrepreneurs and welcome the temporal freedoms afforded by the ride-hailing apps, 'a mediating technology of subordination' (Pollio, 2019: 767) nevertheless impacts their financial freedoms. Thinking infrastructurally about the use and influence of platforms goes beyond thinking digitally. There are emergent, somewhat contingent and co-productive dynamics at work between platforms, urban life and space (Barns, 2019). The aim of this chapter is to explore this in relation to mobility.

Rather than interpreting technology disruption as new, or as a rupture of sorts, I would argue that some forms of continuity are present and that these are particularly pronounced and brittle in the African context. They relate to what exists geographically and materially, as well as the social and institutional structures that form the backdrop to socio-material relations. The question explored in this chapter, and, indeed, in this book, is: does home-grown disruption offer better opportunities for progressive socio-technical evolution? A more specific question would be: does it offer mobility solutions that speak to livelihoods more effectively in African cities?

I investigate possible answers to these questions by exploring empirical vignettes under a number of themes. The first focuses specifically on SafeBoda in Uganda and its own version of what I would term 'endogenous disruption' in Uganda and beyond. Emerging from this example is a web of relations that speak to a relational dimension that stretches across country boundaries. This relates not only to upscaling, but also to context and embedded experiences of technology appropriation. The second example is a closer look at the ride-hailing environment in Nairobi and the emergence of driver-owned apps, such as BebaBeba.

SafeBoda

My first *boda-boda* ride was eventful and somewhat frustrating. The first driver I hailed could not find me due to the absence of a formal street address system in Kampala that allows for accurate pick-up points. Meeting a *boda-boda* rider relies on interpersonal communication via mobile phone and references to local landmarks, despite the Global Positioning System (GPS) functionality of smartphones. I cancelled my trip. My second driver agreed to meet me at the supermarket on the main arterial route nearby. This is a clear landmark near a 'stage', that is, a space where *boda-boda* riders congregate and pick up rides. After putting on the helmet I insisted upon, we were off! My driver expressed concern about the lack of a hairnet, whereas I was more concerned with fastening my helmet properly. Kampala traffic is dense. On the back of a motorbike, one feels vulnerable yet also exhilarated, viscerally aware of motor vehicles passing by within touchable distance. At intersections, there was some light banter and curious looks across the wall of motorcycles as riders waited for the traffic light to change to green and/or the uniformed traffic police officer to indicate that it is permissible to go – I say 'permissible', not 'safe'. None of this felt safe, and yet it did. There is something about the ongoing connection and negotiation that is vaguely reassuring and, well, human. These ruminations of mine at the aforementioned traffic intersection were rudely interrupted by a traffic police officer. My driver was asked to take his bike off the road. His tires were old; he seemed both embarrassed and perplexed at the same time, yet also resigned. There appeared to be some admonition and negotiation, but I was able to hail a third ride. This driver was a little more confident and conversational. The helmet (and hairnet) did not preclude a chinwag while negotiating Acacia Road's traffic, road construction and Ash Wednesday rush to mass. For the equivalent of US$2, I traversed half the city and got a small insight into how mobility works in Kampala. Quick and agile, yes, but a little scary. At the end of the day, I was reluctant to repeat the experience and took an Uber home instead. The cost was three times that of my *boda-boda* ride and took twice as long in similar traffic conditions. My Uber driver was a woman who works as an accountant during the day, with her vehicle providing extra income in the evenings.

When I related my *boda-boda* experience to Ricky Thompson a couple of days later, he used the safety issue as a segue into an account of how he started SafeBoda in 2014. Initially working as a security guard, Ricky became a *boda-boda* rider in 2011 and soon expanded this into *boda-boda* tours for tourists. After he lost a friend in a *boda-boda* accident in 2014, he turned into an advocate for *boda-boda* safety, with the use of helmets seen as paramount. Through this endeavour, he met Maxime Dieudonne and Alastair Sussock, his business partners, and founded SafeBoda. Starting with 150 drivers in 2015, there are now 19,000 drivers in Kampala alone.[2] According to Deepa Shekar, the company's COO, the issue of safety and the associated stigma associated with *boda-boda* riders were the two motivating forces that led to the establishment of SafeBoda. The two issues are related. *Boda-boda* riders are generally seen as irresponsible, aggressive and a danger on the roads. Many of them end up in hospital.[3] No doubt informed by what Doherty (2017: 195) refers to as the industry's allure of urbanity, mobility and subaltern charisma, the SafeBoda app is intended to add a sheen of professionalism through technology (see Figure 3.1). With 'ride' being the core of the business, the SafeBoda platform has enabled diversification of app-based services. These include package delivery, access to insurance and finance, and the sale of airtime. Recently, the addition of food delivery has expanded the business model to include other forms of informal work: the preparation of food by local vendors.

Initially titled *Kya'kulya Chakula* (Swahili term meaning 'food for every day'), the expansion to food services is significant. Expanding services to local food producers, some of whom work from two cloud kitchens, provides *boda-boda* riders with additional income during off-peak hours. Enabling this continuous flow of business is essential to rider livelihoods, as confirmed by Shekar. By broadening this web of actors, the app platform enables the partnering of complementary services in a quantifiable and formalized framework with some financial predictability. What may appear

Figure 3.1: *Boda-boda* riders waiting for a ride

Source: Photograph by author

to be a professionalization of the informal economy is an actual construction of a frame for connections that enable livelihoods. The essential difference here is that the platform is home-grown and contextually embedded. Upon further probing, it emerges that there are deeper, perhaps inadvertent, connections to place.

Place, space and material considerations

A core part of the *boda-boda* physical and institutional network is the 'stage'. As physical hubs that host 15–20 riders, stages represent catchment areas for *boda-boda* riders, with the leadership of each stage elected by its riders and connected to a *boda-boda* association. The latter provides the connection between the riders and local authorities (Howe, 2003). As a system of self-regulation, in some country cases, informed by a legacy of rural cooperatives and welfare organizations (Ibrahim and Bize [2018] refer to Kenya in this regard), the stage provides some form of social solidarity and institutional security. A riding app disrupts this hub-based system, as riders are able to fill their time with rides and deliveries from anywhere, which, in turn, according to SafeBoda respondents, could lead to a more efficient pricing system. Disrupting this system will no doubt have ramifications because the stage is the kingpin of an evolved system of management and accountability among *boda-boda* riders. As described by Doherty (2017: 196):

> The stage system not only generates intense camaraderie among drivers, but is also seen as a way of building trust and accountability both among drivers and between drivers and the public. Stages are seen by drivers as a mechanism to ensure discipline in the industry. Their elected chairmen enforce self-designed codes of conduct, resolve conflicts between drivers, and represent their interests to local government officials. Stages are socio-material landmarks that position and link drivers, passengers, roads, traffic, and multiple forms of regulation. They stabilize the industry by carving coherent and continuous workspaces from the ever shifting world of traffic, providing a sense of security for both drivers and passengers.

Stages are fairly ubiquitous across East African cities and provide some form of spatial reference for customers: walking to a stage and hitching a ride is straightforward and does not rely on the use of precious mobile airtime (see Figure 3.2). What SafeBoda introduces, however, is a more individualized system with a broader catchment area that enables incomes on return rides also. The question, then, is whether the platform entails an expansion and reordering of space.

Figure 3.2: A *boda-boda* stage in Kampala

Source: Photograph by author

While the tendency is to see digital disruption as a market effect with indirect broader impacts, the proliferation of digital platforms requires more careful consideration within the urban realm. There is the articulation with socio-economic vestiges of place, but the material dimension is also significant when considering the precarious nature of gig work in the mobility sector. As Doherty (2017: 193) argues: 'Boda bodies do not simply use infrastructure, but become a substantial component of it.' As a 'critical supplement' to Simone's (2004) notion of 'people as infrastructure', Doherty emphasizes the infrastructure violence that *boda-boda* riders are subjected to as their bodies, livelihoods and labour co-constitute mobility systems. In the Uber example explored by Pollio (2019: 766) in Cape Town, the platform economy's self-employment regime essentially places drivers as supply infrastructure through the social networks that expand Uber's market.

More broadly, digital platforms have become a banal part of everyday urban life, and their impacts are inherently spatial. As part of the assemblages of material, human and data, they are profoundly impactful. What distinguishes SafeBoda from Uber, of course, is that its intention is to grant more agency to riders. Speaking to staff, I was struck by the larger substantive goals that guide them: enabling mobility, traversing traffic congestion and consolidating livelihoods. How these impact on the spatial distribution of stages and their place-making qualities remains to be seen. This informal system of paratransit governance is in need of an upgrade, according to SafeBoda. This expands the notion of disruption as more than a market effect, but an impact that could potentially lead to a sociocultural reorientation, with specific place-based effects. Disrupting the stage system is about addressing perceived market inefficiencies, but it may also destabilize established means of management that some view as exploitative (Howe, 2003). These locally evolved networks can, of course, also be harnessed towards challenging corporate disruption, as shown in the following section.

Nevertheless, the platform logic that accompanies the use of apps does overlay on other forms of economic and social kinship networks. This is not simply a function of one form of organization replacing another; rather, they function in milieus where social infrastructures operate as extensions of material relations and coexist with established 'ways of doing and knowing' (Doherty, 2020). Using the notion of 'personhood' as entry point for considering the layers of socio-technical interaction that emerge from the many interfaces between platform and more traditional logics, Doherty (2020: 8) concludes: 'personhood is not a monolithic, singular socio-cultural form, but is constituted within a complex moral landscape comprised of multiple, unevenly sedimented, historical layers'. The extent to which platforms become part of the everyday would depend on how well these layers are negotiated and the practices that exist. Some doubt is, then, cast on how innovative platforms are. I would contend that this would depend on the definition of innovation. My argument would be that the digital realm is not centre-stage to innovation, but an expansion of opportunities for imagination and appropriation.

Disruption from within

The drive from Nairobi's Jomo Kenyatta Airport to Kibera takes one along the recently constructed bypass intended to ease the city's congestion woes. My Uber driver had much to say about the joy of not spending many expensive hours wasted in traffic. John[4] was taking me to Kibera, where I was meeting with MapKibera, an offline and online mapping platform intended to enable spatial legibility in one of the country's most dense informal settlements (Odendaal, 2018), an initiative I discuss in Chapter 6. As I have found in so many of my travels, it is often what happens en route that provides insight into city dynamics and smart futures.

The conversation started with my observation of the range of ridesharing options in Kenyan cities. Besides the usual suspects – Uber, Bolt and Lyft – there is Little Cab and, more recently, ShareCab, a local rideshare service that does not take commission from drivers, but relies on an annual subscription for operations. LittleCab's advantage is that it is owned by CraftSilicon, a multinational technology firm with headquarters in Nairobi, and Safaricom, the largest telecommunications provider in Kenya and one of the most profitable companies in the East and Central Africa region. As the initiator of M-Pesa, the revolutionary mobile money app launched in the early 2000s, the integration of mobile money and ride hailing was seamless (Wainaina, 2016). While Uber was initially the most ubiquitous ride-hailing app in Kenya, decreasing revenue due to the increase in the numbers of drivers and the addition of Taxify (now Bolt) meant that drivers suffered diminishing incomes. ShareCab emerged as a reaction from ride-hail service drivers. In reading their marketing literature, what distinguishes the local apps is that they focus on three principles: local ownership, a simplified user experience and the integration of local mobile money apps.

This was the theme of my conversation with the Uber driver: dissatisfaction among drivers and growing frustrations at being losers in the technology innovation game. Drivers wanted a sense of ownership and expressed a need to market their own platform.[5] Enter BebaBeba (meaning 'carry-carry' in Swahili), a ride-hailing service initiated by the Drivers and Partners Association of Kenya (DPAK). Ironically, what was essentially a reaction to Uber was also inspired by Uber; in John's words: "Like Uber, we started on the street, not the office." BebaBeba was launched in December 2018 (two months after our conversation), with the following statement by DPAK best encapsulating driver frustrations: 'We have been subjected to losses each and every day, we have lost our vehicles through auction because we can't afford to repay them and some of our friends have lost their lives because of long driving hours' (Durodola, 2018).

At the time of the app launch, there were 2,300 member drivers and a 15 per cent commission was payable by drivers (compared to Uber's commission at the time of 25 per cent), with a KES25 (approximately USD 0.21) per kilometre base fee payable to drivers. The marketing message emphasizes driver sovereignty and ownership.[6] Driver ownership is particularly important. In Kenya, a large majority of ride-hail drivers are hired by car owners, who are actual partners with the taxi-hailing companies. Most owners give the drivers daily targets instead of paying them a fixed salary from the daily collections. Insurance companies, app providers and financial institutions also require to be paid from what is left (Achuka, 2018). Jointly owned by drivers and partners in what developers call 'shareholding', changes to the pricing structure and rider conditions are subject to consultation with DPAC members, introducing new terms and conditions that address drivers' demands. The service has since been expanded to include carpooling, car rental and tourist trips; they also provide a business account portal for corporates. As the most recent addition, the carpooling scheme is an app-based system than connects qualifying car owners with car rental companies.

The corporate assemblages that have emerged from rider platforms hint at a localized set of practices becoming increasingly embedded in local commercial networks. Universal rules of the market have limited application. The assumption that those entering the gig economy are entrepreneurs in the making is precarious at best. The sociocultural contexts within which economic relations are embedded have an impact on driver rights – the global entrepreneur does not exist, only local interpretations of worker access and rights (Firmino et al, 2019). These 'entrepreneurs of sharing' are not necessarily equal partners (Pollio, 2019). BebaBeba seeks to be the exception to that.

Pollio (2019: 760), through a focus of Uber in Cape Town, shines a light on the transparency that enables drivers to escape corruption through 'forms of technological liberation from existing labour arrangements'. Drivers' opportunities to appropriate the means of labour through their own 'hacks' speak to ongoing forms of capital mobilization and immobilization. My Nairobi Uber driver, John, explained how drivers can move between platforms as they fill their time and gently hinted at means whereby riders can be convinced to switch to platforms more amenable to driver needs.

The need for investor capital is a substantive issue, however, as reflected in recent posts on BebaBeba's Twitter account looking for investors for a vehicle rent-to-own programme. The material elements of rider platforms extend not only to the physical impact on space; beyond the algorithms are also the logistics that require the management of the network elements across space, that is, cars, drivers, passengers and payments. As pointed out in online Kenyan publication *Techweez* by Wainaina (2016):

> The smaller players will have to seek ways to manage their logistics much more efficiently. Typically, they should ask themselves how they would lower the arrival time once a rider hails a taxi? How do they ensure even distribution of their drivers? How do they make the process of payments faster and more seamless? What interesting technology will likely attract users to their service? A re-evaluation of these aspects will then likely inform their decision to continue seeking market share or opt out.

While this may be a formidable prospect for local start-ups, another form of disruptive hacking, I would argue, is the very diversification required to stay competitive in this growing market. These are often uniquely local and specific to place-based needs. In the popular press, they are listed as innovations. A timely example (at the time of writing this during the COVID-19 pandemic) is Little Cab's offering of ambulance services. Partnering with St John's Ambulance services, the app offers the Little Rescue category within it, which enables customers to get connected to a St John Ambulance dispatcher, who will coordinate the emergency response with the ambulance crew. Much like their rides can be tracked in real time, the same can be done with ambulances. Speaking on the new partnership, Fred Majiwa, Head of Programme, Business Development and Communications at St John Ambulance Kenya, said:

> This is a timely partnership that will enable Kenyans in dire situations to receive quality emergency care and evacuation in record time.

Customers can now track in real-time an ambulance that has been dispatched to help them, thanks to the live map that has been created. The crew will only need to use one live map to direct them to the emergency scene, which reduces time spent consulting the customer over the phone or use of different maps. This service also helps enhance our management of COVID-19 cases, which we are currently attending to free of charge, as part of our CSR [corporate social responsibility]. (Quoted in Kahende, 2020)

The preceding quote incorporates many aspects of platform urbanism as it relates to the temporal and spatial fixtures of cities. It speaks to the function of technology convergence and the centrality of platforms to urban life. As a 'form of techno capitalism that entails a diverse, on-demand workforce' (Pollio, 2019: 761), the co-constitution of platform structures and urban space through a deepening of the geospatial dimensions of the platform economy (Söderström and Mermet, 2020) represents a different style of platform formation, with geographically distinctive approaches within the same platform (Stehlin et al, 2020).

Relational disruption

Emerging out of the preceding discussion is a regular mention of partnerships, collaborations and networks. The genesis of SafeBoda is an example of how informal networks seeded this ride initiative. My discussion with Ricky Thompson revealed a friendship with the other two founders, enabled through a *boda-boda* tourism initiative and then solidified through the formal establishment of SafeBoda. Thompson referred to the 'strategic partnerships' necessary to enable expansion but then made an important point in the press, as well as in my interview with him, about the alignment of values. This joint commitment to something more than market efficiency was echoed in my discussions with Deepa Shekar, the COO, referring to a bigger picture that, according to my discussions, relates to mobility and enabling the informal to become mainstream,[7] or, as Thompson put it, to 'broaden the web for players that aren't connected to the web'.[8]

I am reluctant to attribute too much value to the emphasis on shared principles, but my observations in Kampala and Nairobi around SafeBoda and BebaBeba revealed the foregrounding of substantive issues related to people's lived experiences. As eloquently illustrated by Doherty (2017), the life of the *boda-boda* rider is precarious and intimately enrolled in the material elements of degenerating road infrastructure, congestion and associated danger. The rideshare 'partners' of Nairobi speak of livelihoods and day-to-day constraints in their oppositional practices to mainstream platforms. The marketing tone of BebaBeba on social media emphasizes local pride and Kenyan innovation. Again, it is tempting to over-romanticize these qualities of endogenous disruption, but they simply reflect a more granular engagement with local context. I recall listening to the country head of operations of Uber South Africa at an ICT summit in East London, South Africa, in late 2019, where the presentation's emphasis on job creation and women's empowerment was contextually appropriate in the South African context. There was nevertheless a marketing spin that appeared somewhat contrived. The lived experiences of disruptor participants in Kampala and Nairobi were represented in an unrehearsed way. What emerged strongly was a spontaneously socio-technical spin whereby the technical, political and material were interchangeably discussed. This was particularly discernible when discussing SafeBoda's expansion into the rest of Africa.

How mobile platforms travel

On the day I interviewed Deepa Shekar (in March 2020), SafeBoda was launched in Ibadan, Nigeria. When I probed her on how it may look different in the West African context, she spoke of: the regulatory landscape being more complex in Nigeria; a local banking system that is sophisticated and allows for credit more readily (which is important when designing the app); investor appetites wakened by the captive Nigerian market; and local smartphone use rates and skills. In Nairobi (launched earlier), users were found to be more tech savvy and the mobile money app M-Pesa is deeply integrated into commercial systems and lifestyles, while the uptake of e-commerce could push the continued rollout towards parcel delivery systems, with local innovator Sendy (delivery app) being the main competition in this regard. Partnering with complementary services that respond more readily to the local character of place makes sense, according to Shekar. The point is to respond to a common problem in most African cities – the inconvenience of accessing food, making payments and getting around town – in a way that fits with local socio-technical conditions. As Shekar put it: 'We believe in what we are doing; Africa needs a localised option.'[9]

The SafeBoda upscaling and expansion initiative reveals a granular approach enabled through an adaptable platform. Pollio's (2019: 768) discussion of Uber in Cape Town highlights the role of the software in enabling local narratives and economic assemblages to shape themselves in accordance with the city's macroeconomic aspirations: 'Through these "partner companies", Uber not only outsources some of the mechanisms of control that contribute to the subjectification of the drivers, but also better intersects local economic networks.' The SafeBoda experience reflects the need to be cognizant of local economic networks, sociocultural impulses and technology uptake. In Nairobi, the challenge is to convert a *matatu* market into a *boda-boda* market or convince the middle-class car driver to convert to using *boda-bodas* given the city's horrendous traffic congestion, whereas in Kampala, the challenge is seen as converting an offline to an online market. Smartphone penetration is low and the relative cost of data is high: 'People do not understand how much they can do with their smart phones', were Thompson's words.[10] Smartphone use in Uganda is low and the use of the app is slowly growing, while the Kenyan market is seen to be more responsive, as the platform finds its place in the 'Silicon Savannah'. Payment in Kenya is enabled through the ubiquitous M-Pesa, whereas mobile money in Uganda is not yet an acceptable form of payment due to convoluted banking regulations and slow adoption rates.

Why SafeBoda chose to expand its operations to Ibadan, not Lagos, the largest urban agglomeration in West Africa, needs reflection. The use of motorbikes for transport was banned in the Nigerian metropolis in February 2020, with the overwhelming official reason given being safety. A public ferry service has been implemented along its waterways, run by Uber and other private sector companies (Salaudeen, 2020). Besides the shock to rider livelihoods and transport costs to commuters, the replacement mode is hardly affordable or practical. The assumption that residents are willing and able to pay for this convenience hardly accords with consumer profiles. The relationship between government regulation and technology disruption is therefore an important theme to explore.

Regulation vacuums and innovation

Digital platform-driven infrastructure, such as Airbnb and Uber, are difficult to regulate and predict. The inherent conflicts within platform urbanism are as much a function of the banality of platforms becoming a part of our daily lives as they are of the control platforms firms have over data and code (Söderström and Mermet, 2020). Technology innovation disrupt both markets and regulatory regimes. In addressing mobility issues, however, this issue cannot be neglected, as some form of replication of and integration with current systems is necessary to impact at scale. In Kenya, rideshare drivers provide a motivation for the Kenyan government to declare ride-hailing companies as transport providers, rather than technology companies, in taxation and regulation, following steps in Europe to do so. However, questions are often raised about the appropriateness of existing regulatory tools.

My discussion with SafeBoda revealed a more dynamic and interactive stance towards regulation based on ongoing interaction, proactive lobbying and political pressure. As Thompson put it: "For us as the innovators, we are always ahead of the regulation." The regulation vacuum is seen as an opportunity to influence measures that allow for growth. Implicit in my discussions in Kampala, though explicitly explored by Goodfellow and

Titeca (2012: 264), is the extent to which *boda-boda* riders form a political constituency in a context where local political power sits with the political opposition: 'Increased political competition has created an environment where informal groups seeking to protect their livelihoods can tactically leverage a presidential intervention in their favour, helping them evade the policies and regulations of the City Council.' As Thompson put it: 'Once they allow you to grow and network; you have power. When you have people who believe in you, then you are very dangerous.'[11] However, the overall message is one of ongoing networking: finding the right political champions, staying in touch with the news and anticipating any policy changes that may impede the work of drivers.

What emerges is a very interactive dance between regulators and SafeBoda, with the platform intended to provide drivers with the technological capital to professionalize and promote road safety. I had encountered this stance before. In work I had done previously on the use of drones in African cities, I found a similar sentiment expressed in Tanzania and South Africa. While the latter chose a rigid regulatory approach, using civil aviation legislation to control the commercial and personal use of drones, what was seen as a regulatory vacuum in Tanzania provided an opportunity for use by collaborative frameworks (for more about this, see Chapter 3).[12] The relationship between innovation and regulation is often seen as one infused with tensions, and the space opened up for negotiated regulation is as much a political process as it is administrative.

Conclusion

In this chapter, I have explored disruption and mobility. Rather than focus on digital disruption as a technical and market-driven process, I engaged it as a continuous process of emergence and remaking. In Chapter 2, I explored the need for a lens that allows for heterogeneity, postcolonial readings of technoscience and encounters with everyday urbanisms. My approach in this chapter, the first of the substantive chapters containing examples of digital disruption, was to explore the role of place and human agency in ongoing socio-technical change. The empirical vignettes were intended to provide material to explore some of these ideas. In conclusion, this chapter opens up the exploration into the dynamic between endogenous technology innovation and substantive urban changes.

Infrastructural systems are susceptible to new factors and actors enrolled in their functioning. What platform urbanism does is decentralize the spheres of influence. The impact of digital disruption on mobility systems is underpinned by a number of factors: how well it integrates with existing systems, user update and, of course, the regulatory environment. In many ways, it requires attention to the contingency of technology and the potential range of relationships produced in what Furlong (2010) refers to as a less centralized view of infrastructure access. Specifically, by enrolling users in the ongoing functioning of the infrastructural space, they are also associated with the performance of said network and can therefore influence it (Furlong, 2010). Infrastructure systems are less stable and predictable than traditionally conceptualized. The examples show that in the mobility terrain, this can also challenge policy in the ongoing dance between disruption and regulation. The reading of power as diffuse and relational (Lawhon et al, 2014: 508), as well as a product of assemblage formation as the material and human are intertwined in place, creates opportunities for a decentred approach to the study of smart disruptions.

The importance of place is an important feature here because it is so blatantly contrary to corporate representations of smart cities and speaks to embeddedness and situatedness. The examples in this chapter show how the notion of place is foregrounded in a number of ways as disruptions travel and are applied elsewhere. The idea of surfaces – 'exposures, folds, hooks, relays, hinges, soldering and shifting parts' (Simone, 2010: 364), not necessarily all manifesting in the same geographic place – reminds us that place-based manifestations are often tied to other spaces. Guma's (2019) work in Nairobi refers to 'fractured constellations', as the spatial impacts of infrastructure constellations are unevenly distributed, and this resonates when considering the many actors active in the ride-hailing domain. Uncovering the dynamic of place requires different questions to be asked, with technology appropriation being approached as a complex practice of translation and appropriation. Blanket solutions and blanket readings of infrastructure systems (Lawhon et al, 2018), or, indeed, undifferentiated framings of platform urbanism, risks the loss of nuance in analyses of urban change. Philip, Irani and Dourish (2012: 9) refer to 'hybrid knowledge practice' as a frame for comprehending power, history, identity and epistemology in understanding socio-technical change. This chapter aimed to begin this exploration by foregrounding how disruptive practices can embed, and can travel, and what their landings entail.

The cultural vertices of place are sometimes indiscernible, and seemingly more so when considering the relationship between place and digital technology. The 'placelessness' of smart city visions gives the impression of neutral territories upon which technology solutions can be superimposed. The poignancy of mobility within this dynamic can simply not be underestimated. Mobility enables movement across space but is also deeply implicated in the configuration of streetscapes and the interconnected, experiential dimensions of the urban. The *boda-boda* riders (and drivers), clutching their cellular phones to their chins while negotiating Nairobi's and Kampala's notorious traffic and potholes, as well as the sale of airtime and associated services at street kiosks, are ubiquitous but also have specific characteristics. Fruit vendors and *boda-boda* riders compete for the same public roadside space, and being a pedestrian exposes you to many offers of contemporary mobility and street side nutrition. The African smart city exists already but looks very different from mainstream visions. Technology appropriation is intrinsically linked to livelihood strategies and lifestyles, as disruption contributes to and enhances the ongoing and unique unfolding of activities in specific urban spaces. The expansion of SafeBoda beyond Uganda and the evolution of the rideshare industry in Nairobi are examples.

This begs the question: does home-grown disruption offer better opportunities for progressive socio-technical evolution? Put differently, can the appropriation of technology at the fringes lead to substantive change? What emerges from the focus on mobility here is that solutions may very well come from the margins but systemic shifts require tweaking from many directions. Furthermore, there is no blueprint for upscaling or replication. Underlying much of the language that I encountered in looking at mobility was a sense of urgency and frustration at the lack of meaningful change.

One of the most tangible urban challenges that emerged during the COVID-19 pandemic was the perpetuation of food security. Inefficient value chains and income inequality are factors, but the pandemic surfaced how urgent these issues are. Chapter 4 addresses this more directly in probing technology in relation to food security and climate change.

4

Digital Food Dialogues

The travels of a banana

In a CNN interview in November 2019, Peter Njonjo, Chief Executive Officer (CEO) of Twiga Foods in Kenya, revealed some startling facts about the journey of a banana. In Europe, the fruit travels 4,000 km from Latin America to a shelf in a supermarket and costs a dollar. A banana in Kenya travels about 300–400 km within the country and will cost the same dollar.[1] His business partner, Grant Brooke, gave a succinct summary of the connection between technology and food:

> The main reason markets do not work here is because there lacks a proper market infrastructure to support the 5 million population in Nairobi. As a result, produce goes bad and there are massive delays at the markets. This means that the cost of the same gets passed to the customer. ... The cost of a banana in Nairobi which has come from Meru or Taveta is the same as the price of a banana in London, which has come from Guatemala. ... This fundamental flaw points to an inefficiency that only technology can solve.[2]

In this quote from an online interview, what becomes apparent is the role of technology in enabling real-time connection, which has positive implications for the management of the food value chain. However, what is also implied in this example is the central role that infrastructure plays in the distribution of food. Thus, the connection between the urban infrastructure that underpins the flow of goods or services and the digital infrastructure that enables flows of information and data will be explored in detail in this chapter. Food serves both as a lens to do so and as an extension of the concerns surrounding climate change given the primacy of the issue of food insecurity as a consequence of global warming. The disjuncture in the cost of two bananas described by Brooke and Njonjo reveals many facets of the growing food crisis in African cities, recently worsened by

COVID-19. According to Njonjo, Brooke and others, the problem is the food value chain and the economic relations associated with that. However, it is also apparent that the last mile of the distribution of products becomes increasingly difficult when urbanization continues without the up-to-date infrastructure to keep up with population growth rates. As argued by Plantin et al (2016), platform and infrastructure studies are two areas of enquiry that are becoming increasingly intertwined as applications become embedded in urban space or, at the very least, impact the ways cities look and function. I believe that food is a convenient lens to better understand such relations.

Chapter 3 examined how disruptive practices in mobility systems are impacted by place-based dynamics. When considering how an app 'lands' in different city and country contexts, it becomes evident that the regulatory environment, local cultural attitudes to technology and the extent to which the platform interfaces with other 'ways of doing' impact how an app is accepted, appropriated and expanded upon. When considering food security, the role of place in the value chain is informed by land use, investment dynamics and the regulatory environment. In the African context, insight into the role of the informal economy in relation to food security is critical. The interface with digital platforms is an emphasis of this chapter. The following section examines this background more carefully in highlighting some of the issues that technologies try to, or could, solve. The centrality of value chain inefficiencies in relation to the spatial qualities of African urban places is explored by examining in more detail the example of Twiga, referred to earlier. Reference is also made to other initiatives that are used, or have emerged, in other parts of the value chain.

Inefficiencies in the value chain result in increased costs for the consumer. The impact on household budgets is profound. Overcoming place-based and infrastructure inefficiencies and dealing with the tyrannies of spatial inequalities of these processes emerges as important. The COVID-19 pandemic was depressingly effective at surfacing the livelihood impacts of spatial inequalities in Cape Town. This impacted on not only the distribution of food, but also production and retail. The imposition of a hard lockdown in South African cities in March 2020 had a profound impact on informal and small-scale food vendors. This, in turn, impacted on household food security. In this regard, the focus of this chapter is on the CTT initiative in the city, aimed at connecting communities and enabling community-based solidarity and outreach. I focus on the CANs formed in response, particularly the emphasis on community gardens, food parcel distribution and other mechanisms used to assist poorer households in accessing food. There are other initiatives mentioned that foreground digital platforms in enabling the equitable distribution of nutrition.

While community gardens proliferated during lockdowns in South Africa and elsewhere, the longer-term concern of the climate crisis is the impact on farming. South Africa and Zanzibar are sources of vignettes for understanding the need for resource protection and efficiency within urban boundaries. The chapter concludes on the recurrence of urban activism enabled through social media platforms in enabling food security, opening space for a more focused exploration of livelihoods and mobilization in Chapter 5.

Food security in African cities

There is some variation in food systems across the continent, but the consensus is that while there may be ample supply of locally grown fruit and vegetables, in general, capacity to produce at scale, as well as the cost of storage and distribution, often frustrate efforts at ubiquitous supply. Food security is about more than hunger, and food production happens across scales and settlement typologies. Physical and economic access to nutritious and safe food to lead a productive and healthy life (how the Food and Agriculture Organization [FAO] defined food security in 1996) remains elusive for many Africans. Food security depends on broader interventions that speak to city systems and infrastructure. Conversely, developmental goals are almost impossible to achieve if household nutrition is not addressed.

Food security is becoming increasingly an urban challenge. The focus on policy shifts has been to ensure that policymakers and funders understand that household food access is situated within a larger institutional and economic context, including retail systems, urban infrastructure and food in relation to external shocks (Smit, 2016). The intersection with cities is therefore an important focus, as the composition of food ecologies are impacted by land-use planning, infrastructure distribution, the relationship of the state to informality and green systems protection, as argued by Battersby and Watson (2018a). The food system forms part of an intersection between urban governance, private investment and distribution infrastructure.

When reflecting on the role of the state or, more broadly, the relationship between governance and food, the relationship emerges as increasingly complex. Research in medium-sized African cities (Epworth in Zimbabwe, Kitwe in Zambia and Kisumu in Kenya) finds that while food insecurity is informed by income poverty, broader urban issues, such as access to water, sanitation and energy, are critical.

Using the Household Food Insecurity Access Scale (HFIAS)[3] to measure the extent of food insecurity demonstrates its high incidence in sampled households, with 71 per cent of surveyed households in Kisumu, 88 per cent in Epworth and 90 per cent in Kitwe being moderately or severely food insecure (Crush and Riley, 2018). This supports findings in other African cities, such as the pro-poor African Food Security Urban Network (AFSUN) surveys, which found high levels of food insecurity in poor neighbourhoods in Cape Town (80 per cent), Lusaka (94 per cent) and Harare (95 per cent) (Crush et al, 2012).

The issue of nutrition transitions in households relates to the availability and cost of foods as external or contextual circumstances change. In many cities, especially in South Africa, nutrition transitions are influenced by the spread of supermarkets, as they reshape supply chains. According to Battersby and Watson (2018a), spending patterns show that households favour local markets for daily and small purchases, and favour large markets, supermarkets and wholesalers for less frequent, large purchases. Spending habits are therefore modified to fit daily household strategies and are impacted by broader urban factors, such as transportation options and household cooking conditions. Supermarket expansion in African cities is impacting food security or, at the very least, the distribution of food. In South Africa, for example, retail is dominated by the 'Big Five' supermarket chains that have expanded into traditional townships. This has been accompanied by a supermarket culture, with fast-food chains often playing a pivotal position in these spaces. Research shows that this has impacted on household dietary choices (South African Urban Food and Farming Trust, 2020).

While economies of scale are assumed to impact on the price of goods, they have sped up the nutrition transition, making cheaper, branded and processed foods more accessible financially. Pricing structures impact on the accessibility of different categories of food, with cheap, instant sources of substance lacking in nutrition and nutrition-rich foods often unaffordable to poor households. Thus, household incomes do not impact nutrition access alone; rather, it is part of a larger systemic issue. Informal traders still tend to stock more fresh produce (Joubert et al, 2018). To some extent, this is due to the lack of refrigeration facilities and the nature of local markets, where household buying patterns tend to be on a cash basis and budgeting on a day-to-day basis.

Existing evidence suggests that food sourced informally makes a significant contribution to energy and protein intake. Steyn et al (2014) review 23 studies, the majority of which were conducted in Africa (Kenya, Nigeria, Ghana, Benin, Mali, South Africa, Uganda and Burkina Faso). They found that the daily energy intake from what they call 'street foods' in adults ranged from 13 per cent to 50 per cent and in children from 13 per cent to 40 per cent. Similarly, they calculated that street foods contribute significantly to the daily intake of protein, often reaching 50 per cent of the recommended daily allowance (Steyn et al, 2014: 1). From a public health perspective, they conclude that street foods 'should be encouraged' (Steyn et al, 2014: 1). In another survey, 70 per cent of 6,453 households surveyed reported sourcing food from informal outlets (Crush and Frayne, 2011: 799). Despite their impact on the nutritional security of households, food vendors in African cities nevertheless face endless harassment from authorities. Roever and

Skinner (2016), drawing on research conducted in five developing-country cities (including Durban, Accra and Nakuru) to examine the more 'everyday' challenges that street vendors face, demonstrate the livelihood impacts of generalized workplace insecurity, harassment and confiscation of merchandise on street vendors' earnings, assets and time.

Recognizing the role played by the informal sector in relation to food security is therefore essential to understanding household survival strategies as they relate to food. It also necessitates a recognition of its position in food supply chains, as argued by Battersby and Watson (2018b: 6): 'fish in Kitwe and Kisumu travelling from China, eggs at the wholesale market in Kisumu coming from Uganda, and vegetables at the Chisokone Market in Kitwe coming from South Africa'. Focusing on the city and its rural environs, or the city region, as the spatial extent of value chains is simply not representative of how food travels. Connections can stretch across country boundaries in the formal and informal sectors. Focus on production alone, as implied in public policy, is simply not enough. Together with other production-based solutions, urban agriculture is beneficial and can make a difference to immediate household needs but cannot provide the solution: 'Those countries which have formulated national food and nutrition security plans (such as Kenya, South Africa, and Uganda) fail to recognise the magnitude of the challenge, and as result they tend to get caught up in viewing food security as an agricultural and rural development challenge' (Crush and Riley, 2018: 50).

Besides being a function of economic relations, food is inherently political and cultural. Research shows that, up to a point, social networks play an important role. Borrowing or sharing is only possible when neighbours or community members have surplus, and in the current context of high food insecurity, dependence on these social networks is simply not possible. Urban food governance is complicated. As a form of intervention, it is implicit in spatial, economic and land-use policy yet not explicit enough to be addressed succinctly. It impacts the location of the production of food in and around cities, transportation systems within and between cities, and the space occupied by retail (Smit, 2016). Food governance includes decisions on traders, market sites and, of course, mall development – but these decisions are seldom made with food security in mind. The governance of food distribution translates into transport policy for freight and passengers. It requires infrastructure for markets, land-use planning that allows informality, and health standards and enforcement. Intervention by the state implies the maintenance of bulk and reticulated infrastructure, such as road systems and water supply, as well as micro-interventions, such as providing potable water, sanitation and adequate protection from the elements for markets and informal traders for food safety.

The question, then, is how to contribute to a more resilient food system that enables greater diversity across value chains and increases affordability to households. Technology has many entries and many roles to play. As a direct communication and ordering tool as part of the value chain, or as a logistics support mechanism, much has been written about the optimizing potential of digital platforms in connecting customers to source through e-commerce. However, there are specifics to consider, such as the impacts of backlogs in communication and logistics infrastructure, and the distributed nature of retail. The role of the informal vendor is essential to consider. This is where the Twiga story is particularly significant.

Optimizing the value chain: Twiga and Yebo Fresh

> 'These days life is easy: you just take your phone; you place your order to Twiga and you receive your goods the following day. Their bananas are of good quality. They can't be compared to the market ones, and they don't get spoiled.' (Peter Macharia, fruit and vegetable seller, Nairobi[4])

In Kenyan cities, *mama mbongas* ('street traders'), *dukas* ('mom and pop stores') and *kibandas* ('street eateries') form an essential part of the food supply chain. Trading along main roads, at transport intersections and on sidewalks, these men and women sell a large proportion of the fruit and vegetables in Nairobi. As a trader, as implied in the previous quote, the many challenges include predicting sales to ensure that produce is fresh, the trustworthiness of suppliers and pricing control. Storage facilities are rare and, if available, shared.

Twiga aggregates demand from small-scale vendors; as Head of Legal and Admin at Twiga Foods Daniel Ngugi puts in: 'we take this demand to the farmers and offer it to them as markets'.[5] Small-scale farmers, often located in peri-urban areas on small plots of land, have the challenge of finding reliable markets and stable price structures for their produce. By connecting farmers and traders directly, effectively cutting out intermediaries, Twiga uses technology to predict markets and reduce post-harvest loss.

The process is well illustrated in the following process, outlined on the Twiga web site:[6]

1. A supplier signs up to join Twiga through its web site and can download the Soko Yethu app. Twiga issues a purchase order and date of harvest; then, it harvests, cleans and measures produce, and issues a receipt; finally, the supplier is paid within 24 hours.
2. This interim step is not to be discounted. Produce is gathered at a collection centre, delivered to a central processing centre, goes to the packhouse for processing and grading, and then dispatched on over 100 sales routes. It is the physical part of the journey and the one that relies on material infrastructure.

3. The final step of the process initially involved the following: a vendor signs up to join Twiga on the web site, a sales representative registers them onto the system and the vendors place their orders with the sales representative. However, from November 2019, once they have downloaded the app, vendors can now place orders, view deliveries made and make payments.

The simple imagery that explains the process on the Twiga web site belies the layered hybridity of the platform and its systemic features. "When we recruit the farmer to our platform" (as stated by Ayub Mutangili, Senior Agronomist at Twiga Foods) is a telling departure point for explaining the start of an enrolment process that includes business skills transfer and simple agro-processing, as illustrated on the Twiga web site.[7]

The Soko Yethu app is the kingpin or access point for an assemblage of functions that speak to the specifics of small-scale trading. The app alone is not enough, nor is the direct connection between farmer and trader the only advantage of enrolment into the Twiga ecosystem. The exchange of money is largely enabled through M-Pesa, the mobile money function that also gives farmers access to credit. The expansion of the app to include ordering facilities for vendors was accelerated by the COVID-19 pandemic. Due to lockdown measures, sales representatives were unable to consult vendors. To vendors, the disruption of supply impacted income and the ability to access loans to pay for goods. M-Pesa can be used by vendors to pay for produce, and the partnership with financial institutions means that they can apply for loans. Customers get to place their orders and have them delivered to their shops at a competitive price with no additional delivery charges.[8]

Figure 4.1: Food sales and deliveries in Kibera, Nairobi

Source: Photograph by author

Figure 4.2: Twiga application marketing

Source: Twiga web site (available at: https://Twiga.com/)

The platform enables such businesses as *dukas*, home or sidewalk kiosks, and small eateries to enable stock fluidity, apply for short-term loans and enable delivery on site. The process of registration can be done with a simple text message and takes two minutes, as seen in Figure 4.2.

In 2021, Twiga partnered with the East African financial services group Britam Holding PLC in offering to develop business interruption insurance cover dubbed 'Soko Afya' to protect small retailers against income loss in the event that they are hospitalized. It recognizes that vendors operate on a day-to-day basis with very narrow profit margins. By providing a daily cash payout, Soko Afya compensates for loss of income due to hospitalization-related business interruption. The platform's ability to expand functionality and enrol new actors echoes the SafeBoda experience, in that market needs at the margins of the food value chains are easily incorporated into the platform business model. There is clearly a business logic that drives these expansions, or, as Doherty (2020: 8) puts it when discussing SafeBoda, a 'digital personhood' that becomes embedded. However, these interventions are layered onto existing networks and practices that are highly contextualized. What I believe is worth reflecting on is the ability of platform technologies to adjust and expand in response to temporal and spatial disruptions.

The assemblage that is Twiga and its associates goes beyond platform architecture, however. A discussion with Gary Benatar, the CEO of Relog, a logistics distribution and supply chain network firm based in Cape Town, unveiled a discussion that was surprisingly urban infrastructure focused.[9] Relog has partnered with Twiga in building and enhancing its end-to-end distribution network. There are two points that Benatar made that struck me as particularly significant to the theme of this book: the first relates to the critical role played by M-Pesa in enabling a cashless exchange of goods and services; and the second refers to how interconnected the platform as a technical backbone is with the urban infrastructure that supports distribution functions. This results in supply chain logistics carefully informed through an interchange between digital and physical spaces: algorithms that predict market behaviour, as well as data sourced through optimizing the IoT, means that the steps in the supply chain can be modelled and predicted, resulting in increased efficiency and, presumably, lower costs for the consumer. According to Benatar, in this transition from batch systems to predictive analytics that enable consistency and 'real-time' management, data on consumer and buying patterns is gold. A radio frequency identification (RFID) tag embedded in each crate essentially gives it a 'licence plate' that can be tracked and traced as 'inventory in motion'. Patterns can be discerned and incorporated into the prediction of greater efficiency in transportation and distribution.

According to Benatar, the COVID-19 pandemic has exposed the inefficiencies of current supply chains in Kenya (and elsewhere). This is specifically true of Cape Town too. The impact on households has been severe in some areas. Evidence gathered in Cape Town shows how this has impacted particularly harshly on food security in marginalized spaces in the city, especially in townships and informal areas, where the informal sector a source is not only of food, but also of employment. Jane Battersby (2020: 1), a geographer well known for her work on food security in African cities, explains it thus: 'the State's attempts to "flatten the curve" include a set of regulations that demonstrate limited understanding of how the poor access food and an ongoing bias towards large scale, formal food system actors'. The South African Level 5 lockdown measures enabled large-scale supermarket chains to continue to trade, with small neighbourhood shops and informal traders initially prohibited from trading.

The food crisis that ensued catalysed action from NGOs and CSOs in South African cities. Yebo Fresh, a technology start-up that targets former townships in South African cities in the distribution of affordable food, partnered with CSOs to get food parcels to those most in need during this time. The company's mandate is to connect mass supplies with markets in townships and informal areas. Based in Cape Town, the staff compliment grew from six full-time staff to 38 after the outbreak of COVID-19, and deliveries have extended to local *spaza shops*, street vendors, township fast-food restaurants, schools, early childhood development centres, soup kitchens and other organizations.[10]

Spaza shops, the equivalent of the Kenyan '*duka*', are a common feature of South African townships. They are essentially tuck shops, often run from home and, since the early 2000s, many in containers sponsored by mobile phone companies. They generally sell everyday household goods, cigarettes, prepaid mobile airtime and food. A conversation with Simon Peters, Head of Special Projects for Yebo Fresh,[11] reveals some of the practical and physical challenges in catering for these and other businesses in less formal areas in particular. One is a very simple issue: the lack of street addresses. In connecting suppliers with both *spaza shops* and households, the lack of formal addresses can frustrate delivery, despite the added functionality of GPS mapping applications. Nevertheless, Peters acknowledges the ability of a digital platform to be agile in a market that is extremely price sensitive due to insecure livelihoods. By predicting buying patterns and considering cooking styles, using app data to forecast preferences is key to connecting the right suppliers with shops/households.

Another practical issue to consider is the storage constraints of *spaza shops* (many do not have refrigeration) and the dominance of a cash economy. While South African mobile payment applications such as SnapScan and Zapper are popular among the middle classes, both these applications generally rely on a connection to a credit card or debit card associated with a bank account, and are therefore inaccessible to those living in informal settlements or working in the informal economy. South Africa does not have an equivalent to M-Pesa that has the same local uptake and functionality. There are facsimiles, but they simply do not have the reach and functionality. Local banks have developed mobile applications, but nothing to the extent of the ubiquity and cultural acceptance of the Kenyan mobile banking app. Benatar and Peters both raised this as key to understanding how platforms are integrated into food supply chains in different contexts. Both their views are hopeful, however, as the availability of existing high-end market platforms, as well as government apps, could perhaps provide vehicles for expanding fiscal reach and payment options, while also becoming more culturally embedded and accepted. The 'tech-savvy' nature and local cultural disposition of country residents impact the reach and shape of food distribution platforms.

While South African cities are generally better served by transportation and communication infrastructure, from which one would assume that food distribution should follow suit, access to affordable food for poor urbanites is an issue that was catastrophically surfaced by the COVID-19 pandemic. Underpinning this dynamic was the structural qualities of South African urban spaces, that is, the fragmentation of urban form as an extension of spatial apartheid.

Figure 4.3: Yebo Fresh marketing

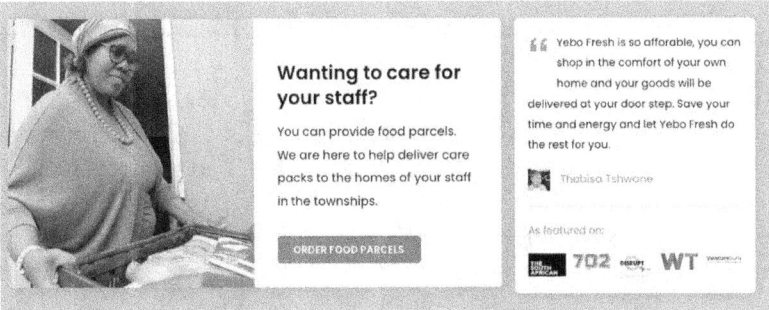

Source: Yebo Fresh web site (available at: www.yebofresh.co.za/)

Food security across space: community action networks

> We were concerned about fellow Capetonians who were not able to prepare for the pandemic by stocking up on food or sanitation supplies. As the lockdown has continued, many families have lost their income. We understand that the need is far greater than the government can provide for, and have chosen to act together. Our response is not to wait, but do what we can.[12]

The hard lockdown imposed on 26 March 2020 following the first COVID-19 cases in South Africa was well intended. Aimed at protecting lives and public health services, the action taken was decisive and swift. What it also displayed was a reckless lack of understanding of how food systems work in marginalized spaces in South African cities. The imposition of a uniform set of regulations across a country of over 60 million people living in settlement typologies that range from remote rural households in traditionally governed areas, to small rural towns, to well-serviced city centres and neighbourhoods, to townships and informal settlements had a tragic impact. The Food Dialogues, a series of talks on several digital and analogue platforms hosted by the South African Urban Food and Farming Trust, focus on South African local food systems, bringing together speakers involved in shaping them. The 2020 series report highlights the deeply systemic and political nature of the South African food system (South African Urban Food and Farming Trust, 2020). The report argues that food poverty was already entrenched before the pandemic, quoting a survey by the African Centre for Cities at the University of Cape Town that found 60 per cent of people in the city unable to afford proper nutrition. The report also picks up on the less direct effects of food poverty and its relationship to the pandemic: 'lifestyle-related' diseases, such as obesity, diabetes and heart conditions, often resulting from a reliance on processed and cheap food products, made this part of the population even more vulnerable to the effects of COVID-19.

The impact of the lockdown was that many people were unable to earn an income to buy food, informal traders were unable to sell food and school food schemes were closed. This resulted in a food crisis that surfaced the vulnerabilities of the wider food system. As Battersby (2020) points out, informal vendors provide food in small, affordable units, with short-term credit to consumers, whereas *spaza shops* are important actors in the food value chain. Regulations were eased to allow for these to function but with very confusing criteria, including the highly contested provision that only South African-run shops be permitted to operate. This was later retracted, but interim enforcement resulted in dire livelihood consequences.

The critical role played by CSOs in enabling the distribution of food during the early days of the lockdown cannot be underplayed. In the Western Cape (the province that Cape Town is located in), in the period from 25 March to 5 June 2020, an average of 41,635 people were fed each day and 77,469 parcels were distributed by CSOs.[13] According to Andrew Borraine, former CEO of the City of Cape Town and now Director of the Western Cape Economic Development Partnership (WCEDP), "This is possibly the biggest revival of civic activism since the 1980s." The legacy of street-level organizing was honed during the anti-apartheid struggle, where bottom-up community-based social support proliferated. Many of these organizers are still active in their communities, responding to challenges of urban poverty and political exclusion.

Shortly before lockdown, a group of medical researchers, public health specialists and activists formed a collective entitled 'Cape Town Together' (CTT) to intervene in what was anticipated to be a public health and humanitarian disaster. Anticipating a 'command-and-control response' from the state, the group understood the shortcomings of a top-down intervention and the impact that could have on marginalized communities. The collective experiences and histories of the individuals in this collective included the Ebola response in West Africa, as well as the 'Fees Must Fall' movement at South African universities. These experiences provided lessons on the limitations of a hospicentric approach to resisting the virus and the efficacy of decentralized mobilization using digital platforms[14]: 'Community intelligence – in other words, the tacit, situated knowledge arising from and produced within life-worlds and lived realities – cannot be compartmentalised into a standard operating procedure' (Van Ryneveld et al, 2020: 2). The pioneers of CTT developed an online toolkit to encourage neighbourhoods to self-organize into autonomous, local CANs. Starting with 14, within two months, there were 170 CANs across the city (Van Ryneveld et al, 2020).

No two CANs are the same; they are developed in accordance with the specific characteristics of their focus neighbourhoods. The CANs built on existing mobilization energies but with sets of values and tools intended to enable self-organizing, neighbourhood-level and community-based responses to COVID-19. There is no hierarchy or central organizing structure; CANs are decentralized, adaptable and collaborative, with each unique in its composition of members and representation from other organizations, such as faith-based groups or street committees. There is a temporal flexibility also: 'New thematic CANs emerge organically on a regular basis in response to emerging needs, and old ones disintegrate as the energy of the group is needed elsewhere' (Van Ryneveld et al, 2020: 2).

Nevertheless, food was and remains a focus. Enrolling local food production and distribution was critical as the food insecurity increased during the hard lockdown implemented in late March 2020. This resulted in a network of community kitchens and food distribution schemes, such as food parcel deliveries, often done under police protection.[15] Again, there is variation across CANs, with home kitchens dominating some areas, while local restaurants closed due to lockdown measures reopened as free community kitchens in others. A food growers' CAN connects small-scale farmers, forming a platform to share knowledge and seeds.

One of the key principles that informs CAN functioning is the notion of 'moving at the speed of trust', where human relationships and social solidarity are seen as motivators to action, rather than preconceived project plans. The network is built on interpersonal relationships: 'the network *is* its relationships'.[16] These values are represented in CTT's 'ways of working' mandate. New forms of community organization emerged, connecting across historical spatial boundaries, with a solid set of principles where connection is the basis of doing and sharing. Storytelling, building relationships and non-partisan partnerships, and adaptive leadership form the bedrock of what is now considered the CAN 'movement'.

The model of organizing is simple and underpinned by digital platform synergies. An online portal allows for registering a new CAN or joining one in proximity to an applicant's home. When the movement started, new CANs were formed through CTT enabling connection through WhatsApp and email, based on similar neighbourhoods and interests. The CAN 'starter pack' provides a resource on COVID-19, safety protocols and guiding principles for working in a non-hierarchical and decentralized way. These 'ways of working' were formulated as a frame for interaction, much of it to avoid the pitfalls of social media and online communication. Digital organizing was key, but as Leanne Brady, one of the pioneers, confirms, the digital divide in relation to data costs and access to smartphones was a definite constraint. Close to R100,000 (approximately US$6,600) was spent on data collectively across the CANs – digital organizing was key, with platforms forming a core part of the organizational infrastructure.[17]

Smart features, mainly in the form of social media, are appropriated in accordance with local needs, but the function of the WhatsApp group is central. How this proliferates into other forms of smart technologies is dependent on the definition of local priorities. Knowledge dissemination reflects place-based histories and resources, with many using the networking capacity of individuals to overcome constraints to movement. This social network of networks is a juxtaposition to the one-size-fits-all state response. Each network formulates its own analysis of what the most pressing issues are and, using local resources, formulates self-organizing neighbourhood initiatives. The 'ways of working' frame is critical to ensuring that misinformation is not spread and that a 'calling-out' culture was avoided. WhatsApp provides a bounded network model which ensures that groups are representative of joint interests. Facebook provides a visual and storyboard platform that was seen to be more widely accessible and useful for keeping the broader public informed, while also providing a starting point for new recruits. Here, the role of moderator volunteers is essential to ensuring the space is safe from trolls and misinformation peddlers.[18]

A partnering model was adopted to enable linking not only within communities, but also across neighbourhoods, reflecting the agility of this modular approach. At the time of writing, there were 12 such pairings. The result has been the sharing of information and ideas, or two-way learning, with food relief being a major emphasis. A radio interview with one such pairing reveals the collaboration, which included fact checking fake news, the transfer of mobile phone data and electricity service top-up payments.[19] Mention is also made of partnering with Uber drivers to enable food delivery within lockdown restrictions.

One such pair includes my own neighbourhood, Sea Point, part of the Atlantic Seaboard, an admittedly 'well-heeled' part of the city that hugs the Atlantic Ocean. The Seaboard CAN partnered with Guguletu, an apartheid-era township that is home to about 25,000 people about 17 km from the central business district and 20 km from Sea Point. Distribution of food, donation of food parcels and working with established outreach food providers, such as Ladles of Love, is a core part of the network's activities. The diversity of neighbourhood needs and the loss of income of 2,000 households in Gugulethu led to the development of the Sinani voucher. The voucher is a simple artefact that is part of an ecosystem of care, including a number of digital platforms. As shown in Figure 4.4, the process combines the efforts of street champions and campaign donations to distribute food to vulnerable households.

The process is mindful of local needs and includes residents in the distribution of vouchers. Platform support is enabled through an online donation system, using Snap Scan, a local mobile payment app, and credit

Figure 4.4: Sinani voucher information

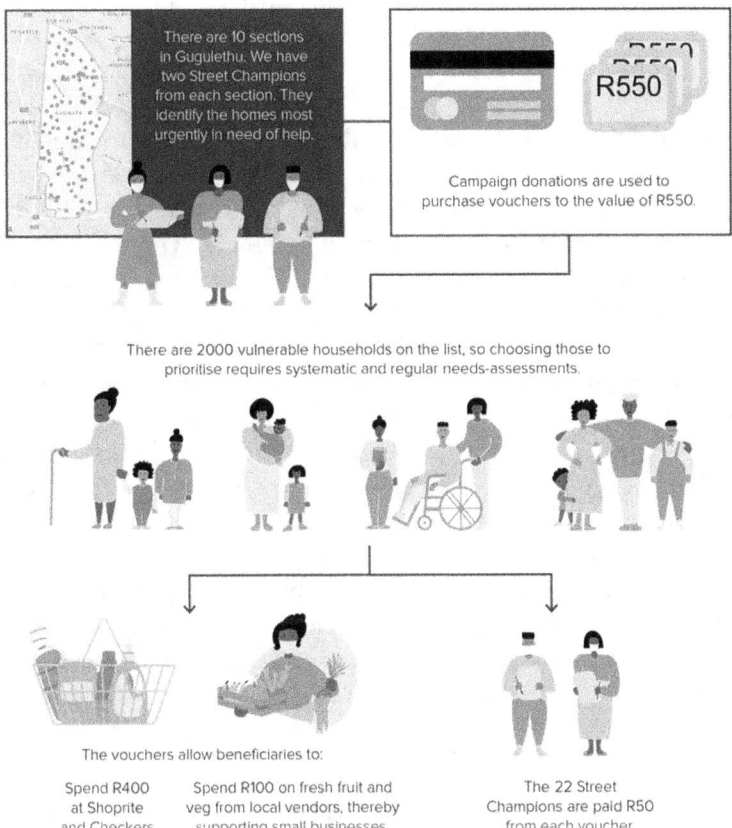

Source: Seaboard CAN web site (available at: https://seaboardcan.org)

card functions, and is extended and organized through WhatsApp. In many ways, the voucher represents a hybrid quality of online and offline assistance.

The advantages of using vouchers, as listed on the web site, include autonomy, discretion, health and safety. They can be customized to suit household needs and can be redeemed at supermarkets or local traders. This flexibility, enabled through technology, is specifically enabled to support small, local businesses, where R100 (about US$7) of each voucher is used to buy fresh produce from local vendors and veggie boxes that are distributed door-to-door. The vouchers and veggie boxes are distributed by 22 local volunteers. Vouchers are traced directly to beneficiaries through ID and mobile phone numbers but are delivered by hand.

A second initiative that emerged from the pandemic is a web dropdown menu item termed 'Food Gardens and Placemaking' on the Seaboard CAN web site. It is an intriguing category because it associates what is ostensibly a rural activity, farming, with an urban planning preoccupation: the making of place. The Gugulethu Urban Farming Initiative (GUFI) is a network of backyard and community gardens created to enable local self-sustainability. They are part of a tradition of urban farmers in Cape Town, a city that was founded in the 1600s as a fresh produce post for passing Dutch East India Company ships. Vuyani Qamata, a member of GUFI, refers to himself as a 'a farmer without land'.[20] He describes how he heard of the CAN initiative on a WhatsApp group with other farmers and on the radio. He describes in an online video how the long history of farming in 'Gugs' is coming to fruition as younger members of the community become involved and bring their expertise and creativity to the process.

Also in the narrative captured on the video is the snowball effect of online or WhatsApp-based organizing, with an expansion of urban farmer networks across the city. Using the phrase 'just start' as a tagline throughout the video, Qamata describes his idea of turning Gugulethu into a food forest. He is not alone in his ambitions. Throughout Cape Town and other African cities, urban dwellers are becoming increasingly food insecure, with the pandemic surfacing these concerns.

Urban gardening is an important contribution to more food-secure households but, as many argue, not sufficient to address food insecurity (Battersby and Crush, 2014). Thus far, I have made little reference to one of the causes of food insecurity: the climate crisis. The impact on crops

Figure 4.5: Urban farming in Gugulethu, Cape Town, in the shadow of a Shoprite supermarket

Source: YouTube video still (available at: www.youtube.com/watch?v=ofuPAbQFyI8)

may appear to be a rural issue, but one of the biggest urban challenges is the increase in the number of food refugees entering African cities. Going back to source and recognizing the interrelatedness between elements of the food value chain across space is important.

Back to source: technology from above

While the distribution of food is key to effective urban functioning, production on urban fringes and in rural hinterlands is key. The use of technology to enable more finely grained prediction and management of crops is very much in vogue. Agricultural technology ('agritech') is an expanding field, with many disruptive technologies impacting on various parts of the food value chain. Krishnan, Banga and Mendez-Parra (2020) define agritech as a combination of hardware, software applications, data chains and learning processes that enable monitoring and evaluation. According to Krishnan, Banga and Mendez-Parra (2020: 27), the use of platforms, succinctly defined as 'Data-connected devices using information and communication technology (ICT), internet and artificial intelligence (AI), primarily driven by software development', is driving e-commerce in agriculture, serving as marketplaces. Knowledge sharing is a feature, as farmers can showcase best practices and post various experiences of participating on agriculture platforms online. Knowledge generation is a key aspect that is influenced by ICT in several ways, as is shown in the vignettes discussed in this chapter.

The Twiga case shows the power of a platform in enabling those on the margins of the food value chain to be included in a way that is honouring and enabling of livelihoods. The CAN example shows how a combination of social media and associated apps (WhatsApp) can build across and within communities, while facilitating resource transfer. The immediacy enabled through digital platforms also engenders contextualized accounts that potentially build on local experience. There is nevertheless a broader overview necessary to enable systemic transitions to more sustainable practices. Climate change events, such as floods, and crop failure due to associated disease events impact on the volume and quality of food production. Urban farming practices are useful but have limitations in relation to their impact on food security. Research in Harare, Zimbabwe, for example, shows that despite tacit acceptance of urban agriculture practices in policy terms, the regulatory environment can be very difficult for urban farmers and frustrate efforts to farm at scale (Toriro, 2018). Crush and Riley (2018: 49) cite several studies which show that a 'productionist' approach to food security has limitations: 'Urban agriculture can be beneficial, but there is little evidence that it is effective in targeting the needs of the most vulnerable urban residents.'

Consideration of the inefficiencies of the food chain is critical to understanding urban food security, but poor resource efficiency and inadequate waste disposal in the operations of that food chain require attention from a sustainable resource management perspective (Sibanda and von Blottnitz, 2018). Reduction of land for food production as urbanization creeps up on peri-urban and rural land is also a consideration in thinking through the food system (Hayombe et al, 2018).

Many of these issues do speak to the need for governance frameworks and associated actions, informed by reliable data, as well as engagement with the impacts of policy decisions on the food value chain. The African Union published a report in 2018 detailing the advantages of using drone technology for agriculture. As a farming management tool, the use of unmanned aerial vehicles (UAVs) to map, predict and plan agricultural production is enabled through embedded sensor technology and associated data applications (African Union, 2018). The report highlights the advantages of using drone technology to map environmental change and thereby monitor climate impacts. This data then inform resilience strategies, disaster management and, of course, forward planning. The report highlights several challenges: technological uptake and availability; economic limitations; social acceptance; and inappropriate or inadequate regulatory frameworks (African Union, 2018: 1). These become more textured when considering the evolution of the Zanzibar Mapping Initiative.

As an East African island, Zanzibar has a very delicate ecosystem, which is also the source of its economic output as a tourism hotspot and agricultural producer for residents' livelihoods. The population is very vulnerable to the rising threat of climate change, as symptomized by an increase in the incidence of natural disasters. Disaster risk management is therefore critical because much of the economy depends on the marine and terrestrial ecosystems. In 2002, agriculture accounted for an average of 34 per cent of gross domestic product (GDP) and provided about 75 per cent of foreign exchange earnings. About 60 per cent of the total cultivated land is planted to food crops.[21]

The Zanzibar Mapping Initiative is an initiative that uses low-cost drones instead of satellite images or crewed planes to create high-resolution maps of the islands of Zanzibar and Pemba, an area of over 2,300 km^2 in extent. The Zanzibar Commission for Lands uses the maps for forward planning, land-tenure mapping and environmental monitoring. The Zanzibar Mapping Initiative is an ambitious mapping project born of a partnership between the World Bank, the Zanzibar Commission for Lands and the State University of Zanzibar. It was modelled after a drone mapping and digitization project called 'Dar Ramani Huria', a Swahili phrase that translates to 'The Open Map of Dar es Salaam'. Using lightweight, yellow-and-black senseFly eBee drones costing US$20,000 each, geospatial technology students from the

State University of Zanzibar conducted a pilot project on Unguja, Zanzibar's larger island, to map the island. The purpose of the project was to create up-to-date spatial data for strategic and political interests in land administration development control. Most importantly, there was an emphasis on resilience planning because it impacts on future food production.

There are two issues that need to be considered when reflecting on these drone experiences: first, cultural buy-in, as the use of drones is seen as highly contentious and people tend to associate them with military use; and, second, privacy and the suspicions related to that. Khadija Abdulla Ali, a certified drone pilot, explains it thus: "In some areas, they fear the drone", Ali said; "They think it's a bomb when it crashes. Or they say, we don't want you to fly drone because you will know our secrets, so you can't." The drone project has enabled women like Ali and her female counterparts to challenge prevailing stereotypes of the role of women on the majority-Muslim Island, a small stride towards closing a gender gap in economic opportunity. Women account for almost three quarters of the agricultural workforce.[22]

The issue that surfaces regularly is around regulation. Lockhart and others (2021) document some of the regulatory and political work that was required to cut through a very complex landscape of laws and regulations in order to ensure that the mapping project could go ahead. The Zanzibar Mapping Initiative began in 2016 and is certainly seen as one of the most celebrated examples of Africa drone innovation. It was able to flourish, in large part, because of government support in a semi-autonomous Zanzibar in relation to Tanzania. Other views are less flattering: "This government has a strongly Soviet bureaucracy – a very Soviet past – and is set up with a central command control structure", Anderson, the World Bank official associated with the project, is quoted as saying. A 2015 law made it illegal for any publication or organization to call data 'official' unless they have been approved by Tanzania's National Bureau of Statistics. Inability to share data and the suspicions surrounding that no doubt impact on broader applicability.

Nevertheless, the high-profile learning experience created by this initiative has not only provided the state with a tool to monitor the impact of climate change and address threats to agricultural production, but also had a sociocultural impact. As Frederick Mbuya, Tanzania's Commissioner for Science and Technology, puts it: 'There is nothing more powerful than a young innovator in Africa building something themselves and it flying.'[23]

Conclusion

Ideas form as problems become clearly manifested and solutions are sought. This chapter has shown that innovation can come from unexpected places yet, upon investigation, reflect how the 'everyday' can extend to the extraordinary. The food industry exists largely in the private realm, but its impacts range from the intensely personal to the very broad public qualities of city functioning. In Zanzibar, an island that is largely urban yet in the immediate vicinity of agricultural resources, remote-image data are used to address the most immediate livelihood concerns. The CAN initiative in South Africa connects the links in the food production chain: urban gardening, the distribution of goods across neighbourhoods and procurement by households. In the discussion of Twiga, Yebo Fresh and CANs, understanding of and sensitivity to the entanglement of the formal and informal are critical. *Mama mbongas, dukas, spaza shops* and *kibandas* are critical actors in ensuring food security at a neighbourhood scale. Platform technology enables connections across spatial barriers and socio-economic boundaries, and, in some ways, it enrols these marginalized contributors into the food chain, an economic network that ultimately impacts households. The COVID-19 pandemic clearly features prominently in this chapter but brings with it accounts of community and social mobilization that are key to future inclusive cities.

Joubert et al (2018) adapt the FAO's guidelines on food security to formulate the following pillars of food security: availability, accessibility, usability, stability and agency. The availability of food is related to production, and two examples in this chapter speak to how technology can assist in that. Social media and WhatsApp groups assist in the proliferation of food gardens in Cape Town: swapping seeds, sharing practices and recruiting new gardeners. In Zanzibar, the technology is used to map and monitor the climatic crisis manifestations that impact food production.

Accessibility is clearly not just a distribution issue. While the physical transfer of goods is reliant on urban infrastructure and storage, the use of app functionality enables a more finely grained approach that allows for the enrolment of street traders, small-scale farmers and small stores into the distribution network. In times of crisis, most pertinently, the COVID-19 pandemic, the use of social media and WhatsApp by neighbourhood groups in the CAN network enabled the delivery of food parcels and, in doing so, collaboration with more established charities and CSOs.

Usability is impacted by the lack of storage facilities for most of these actors. The Twiga app allows for street traders to order when needed and provides some form of prediction when planning. The Yebo Fresh initiative allows for the delivery of a combination of goods that appreciate cultural preferences and is sensitive to storage constraints. Enabling some form of predictability for farmers and vendors in the Twiga ecosystem, and partnering with banks and M-Pesa, allows for stability and some form of safety net when incomes falter.

The last criterion noted by Joubert et al (2018) is an important one in relation to the themes of this book, especially the following chapter: agency. Enhancing the ability of poor households to act and for those operating at the margins of food retail to plan, access finance and communicate their needs is immensely empowering. Growing food and sharing knowledge and resources across rich and poor neighbourhoods are dignified ways of straddling spatial inequalities. Overcoming cultural barriers to access skills related to drone technologies while engaging barriers to food production is illuminating and inspiring to others. The notion of agency is central to the vignettes shared in this chapter. Underpinning the motivations of the creation of these instances of innovative problem solving using platform technology is a strong commitment to livelihood enhancement.

Throughout the CAN case, in particular, the cultural tendencies in South African urbanites towards activism and mobilization are clear. Also emerging are techniques that combine technology tools with a more traditional array of collaboration strategies to maximize the breadth of participation and deepen connection. This mode of activism relies on rational strategizing, much of it in South Africa honed through the anti-apartheid movement, and the use of technology to enable the sharing of subjective interpretations of issues and human experience. Chapter 5 expands on the other elements of livelihoods in African cities and the digitally enhanced mobilization tactics used to address exclusion and survival. The aim is to uncover what these strategies contribute to urban inclusion and how they differ from past interventions from the bottom up. Part of this relates to what qualifies as data and the nature of information. In many ways, it not only considers the stories of the everyday, but also poses an epistemological question as to the nature of knowledge in urban practices.

5

Cyborg Activism

Introduction

> The failures of the past have made us more savvy and more knowledgeable. They should have also made us wise enough to stop claiming that global socio-environmental equality, social welfare or value creation can be reduced to indicators. (Kaika, 2017: 6)

The advent of big data and algorithmic decision making has contributed to an overextended faith in the power of numbers. Referring to the sustainable development goals (SDGs), Kaika (2017) discusses the limitations of indicators in giving true representations of socio-economic well-being and progress in cities. Signals of 'dissensus', identifiable in social mobilization, are perhaps more adept at capturing 'what is not working' through insight afforded by conflict and disagreement (Kaika, 2017). By focusing on what lacks, the spotlight potentially shines on the dysfunction of urban systems and governance, allowing the cracks to show.

I have not been explicit about data in the vignettes discussed thus far, but the nature of knowledge exchange enabled through platforms has emerged as a point of focus. Part of the aim of this chapter is to explore the nature of data and the qualities of knowledge generated through digitally enabled activism. Here, I am particularly drawn to the critique of big data, much of this work inspired by Rob Kitchin and others. The tendency to equate data with a true representation of the city is problematic given the messy work of deliberative democracy and the need for problem solving that is contextually appropriate (Kitchin and McArdle, 2016). Chapter 4 showed how misguided policy around the food system, for example, can impact livelihoods. Knowing the messy city through indicators and aggregating its complexity into an infographic is the ultimate in scientific rationalization and objectification (Kitchin and McArdle, 2016). Ultimately, data are disassociated from identifiable subjects/objects and stripped of context.

Algorithmic governance is productive of subjects and spaces (Kitchin and McArdle, 2016). Indicators are 'assemblages' of human and inanimate agency, rather than objective 'truths' (Kitchin et al, 2015). Reducing and oversimplifying complex relationships into measurable variables decontextualizes the city and assumes replicability across places. Benchmarking across cities (and countries) is an understandable trend in the ongoing 'worlding' of cities (McCann et al, 2013) but runs the risk of duplicating pre-packaged urban 'solutions' based on an analysis that is not mindful of the uniqueness of place. Kaika's call for examining where the cracks are through investigation of oppositional practices is an invitation to engage the messiness inherent to cities.

Oppositional data-driven initiatives have often evolved in response to crises, dramatic policy interventions or events. The oft-cited example of this is the Arab Spring, which illustrated the performative dimensions of ICT. In Egypt and Tunisia, social media played an important role in influencing key debates before both uprisings and assisted in spreading democratic messages beyond the countries' borders, both during and after demonstrations (Howard and Hussain, 2011). ICT was part of broader heterogeneous networks, which included television and radio, and built upon existing social and kinship capital (Allagui and Kuebler, 2011). It is never just about the technology. An important point made by these authors, and an underlying theme of this book, is that these multilayered, technology-mediated exchanges are subject to context, differentiated access and existing social networks. This is evident in the CANs example in Chapter 4. Historical social mobilization strategies influence current approaches to activism, including how platforms are appropriated towards social change. This chapter examines this in more detail by unveiling how a 'politics of dissensus' is engaged through expanded digital platform use.

In preparing Chapters 3 and 4 by perusing online forums, watching YouTube videos of interviews with some of the pioneers of these initiatives, conducting in-person interviews and scouring web sites and social media, I was struck by the predominance of storytelling as a form of communication and outreach. Working in the African urban planning field, I found there to be a cultural resonance between the many African traditions of storytelling and the research methods that build on this sensibility. The study of cities lends itself to engaging the 'everyday', or the lived experiences of urban dwellers. In particular, telling stories through case-study research, creates opportunities for authentic and contextual insights afforded by capturing the many dimensions of a research problem through the detailed examination of a case (Duminy et al, 2014a, 2014b). What I found in the work done towards recording the vignettes in this book is how storytelling as a method of activism and advocacy recurs. Social media enables some of this to become intensely personal at times. The personal touch added by zooming in on the experience of actors, their everyday encounters and the experiential sharing thereof is a means to win hearts and minds. For the researcher, it is also a rich portrayal of the textures of urban life. In this chapter, I am particularly interested in how this technique becomes a tool for mobilization and activism. Specifically, I examine how the many functionalities of platforms enable such embroidery and expand networks of action.

Social media and messaging apps have become a means to organize and mobilize. Together with the usual offline mechanics of activism, the arsenal of digital media available for information dissemination and publicity have been well harnessed towards social justice in many African cities (Mitchell and Odendaal, 2015; Odendaal, 2018). Elsewhere, I have explored these two dynamics as representative of a tension between the post-apartheid state's aspirational digital consensus and the workings of a messy democracy at the margins (Odendaal, 2019). In this chapter, I delve deeper into what I argue is a shift in the knowledge domain of governance discourses. By exploring the landscape of digitally informed social activism in Cape Town, I aim to uncover the performative nature of data appropriation and its implications for African cities.

As mentioned previously, the CAN initiative is a continuation of a culture of mobilization that was refined during anti-apartheid struggles, especially in the late 1980s. It is also informed by more recent struggles that made use of technology, such as the Treatment Action Campaign during the 1990s (Grebe, 2011). South Africa's post-apartheid landscape is replete with reconstruction discourses that place great faith in the state to enable more inclusive and representative cities. As evident in the number of service delivery protests and countermovements, many feel that the state has largely failed the poorest members of its population. Given the country's turbulent history, the focus on social justice is apt and understandable, and the resort to activism is a natural progression. Cities were battlegrounds of (often violent) struggles against the apartheid state during the late 1980s, and the focus was overwhelmingly on the material inequalities represented by skewed infrastructure provision. Today, these struggles continue, and while methods of mobilization rely on established activism networks that were forged in late apartheid years, the digital overlay has brought with it a form of engagement that is a hybrid of online and offline strategies, speaking to a more differentiated public. For this chapter, I have chosen to delve a little deeper into the CAN movement, as well as the activities of NU, a group of activists that use research and strategic litigation to campaign for justice and equality in poor and working-class communities in Cape Town.

Across the continent, interest groups mobilize to address injustice and inequality in cities, perhaps not as forcefully as evident in the South African examples in this book, but with similar intentions nevertheless. Knowledge sharing and generation do emerge as underlying motives in the actions of the CANs, with CTT's emphasis on relying on 'professors of the street' to inform neighbourhood-led networking being an example. The second vignette of this chapter is the collaboration between a number of institutions and community groups in Sierra Leone that work with residents in informal settlements to gather and share data, with the aim of influencing urban policy. Part of this story is about what is referred to as 'pedagogical urbanism' (Berney, 2011), learning and doing, as well as sharing, towards social action. CSOs collect, generate and process data in order to respond to the state's failure in an informed and empowered manner. Capturing, sorting, storing and interpreting data is a form of activism.

The advent of big data and the foregrounding of the processing power of algorithms have shifted much of the smart city literature focus onto data. In 2014, the SDI launched a campaign entitled 'Know Your City' at the World Urban Forum in Medellín, Colombia, as a means of building smart cities from the bottom up. The data-driven urbanist trend is driven by the need for service delivery and political accountability globally. It relates to ongoing dissatisfaction among social groups that are economically and spatial marginalized. The SLURC works with SDI affiliates in this regard. This is an institutional space where policy imperatives are combined with activism, using a hybrid range of digital platforms and on-site activism. As a founding advisory board member, I was taken by the value of engaging policymakers experientially, as well as by the networking capacity of CSOs, including local SDI affiliates.

A slightly submerged theme that I would also like to 'tease' out is the role of digital platforms in capturing and influencing popular opinion through visual means. I offer a more explicit account of one initiative that uses drone technology and photography to illustrate the remarkable inequalities of many African cities. Used as a tool of consciousness raising and perhaps also policy impact, the use of the drone has expanded to include broader social intentions, as we saw in Chapter 4. The aim here is to show how an elevated yet finely grained visual account can capture the public imagination in its representation of inequality. This, then, is the segue into Chapter 6, where the emphasis is on the digital public and their future(s) in African cities.

Cyborg activism in Cape Town, South Africa

'Cape Town is the most segregated city in the world' is a refrain often heard, especially when considering the city's status as an international tourist destination in the midst of extreme urban poverty. Cape Town's strategic vision contained in its long-term spatial planning policy is strongly supportive of inner-city densification (South African cities are notoriously sprawled) and racial integration. Yet, it is also subject to property market trends that undermine releasing well-located land for low-income housing. Its immediate post-apartheid focus on spatial integration was also largely frustrated by institutional restructuring and a convoluted national housing policy that constrained the delivery of well-located social housing (Turok and Watson, 2001). More recently, the city's attractiveness to international property capital has increased the market value of centrally located land and also contributed to the gentrification of formerly low-income neighbourhoods on the fringes of the Central Business District (CBD). The gap between the stated intentions of the city's policies and actual delivery has widened, as spatial plans inadequately consider market trends and property dynamics (Odendaal and McCann, 2016). This has resulted in a very difficult city for poor people to live in; travel times to jobs can be long and transport costs place a strain on household budgets. It is no overestimation to say that the best-located residential areas in Cape Town, with good access to public transport and close proximity to urban amenities and commercial prospects, are occupied by medium- to high-income residents.

In late 2015, the former public school of Tafelberg, located in the Atlantic Seaboard suburb of Sea Point, a high-density, middle- to high-income, mixed-use neighbourhood on the oceanfront, was advertised for sale to a private education company. The public advertisement sparked the mobilization of domestic workers and low-income earners in Sea Point against this, arguing that the city should follow through on its stated policy intentions to deliver social housing on well-located publicly owned land in the city, not sell it to private concerns. Seasoned community organizers teamed up with local interest groups in staging a campaign entitled 'Reclaim the City' (RtC), assisted by NU, a legal and human rights organization. The primary aim of the movement was to stop the sale of the school site. It subsequently evolved to include two campaigns: the first was continued pressure on the municipality to deliver affordable housing on inner-city state land beyond the Sea Point site; the second followed the eviction of tenant families in a gentrifying neighbourhood called Woodstock, also near the CBD, demanding from the City of Cape Town that temporary accommodation be provided in the area.[1]

The campaign oscillated between a steady process of documentation and legal work, and digitally augmented public events and interventions. The employment of the 'spectacle' in enabling emotional connection through the sharing of personal experiences is a significant element of the campaign's public profile and essentially defined its origins. The campaign's tagline, 'Land for People not Profit', soon became a familiar feature in public spaces in Sea Point following the first protest march on 1 March 2016. Ongoing protests at the Tafelberg site were augmented with social media. An examination of the campaign Twitter feed at the time found that a significant feature is the personalization of key actors implicated in the sale: the provincial premier, the first judge appointed to hear the court case in which NU challenged the sale of the site, the leaders of the RtC campaign and national and local politicians.

As is the case with social media, the discourse became uncomfortably personal at times yet succeeded in creating the storylines necessary to convey household struggles against gentrification and the follies of property capital.

The sale of the Tafelberg site was suspended as a result of the public pressure facilitated by RtC and NU, the organizational arm of the campaign. A call for architectural proposals has subsequently displayed the technical viability of social housing for the site. The campaign worked. In August 2020, the Western Cape High Court (the provincial court in Cape Town) set aside the Western Cape Provincial Government's sale of the property to a private buyer for R135 million (approximately USD 8 million), based upon the argument that the province and the City of Cape Town have a constitutional duty to combat spatial apartheid.[2]

The systemic issues that led to the creation of the campaign in the first place still need to be addressed, however, and what was initially a protest against the sale of one site became an ongoing campaign for the reallocation of centrally located public land for social housing. Here, RtC activists took the experiential dimension of the campaign further with the subsequent 'symbolic occupation' of two vacant public buildings in the city.[3] The location of these properties is significant. One is located on the fringes of the Victoria and Alfred Waterfront, a mixed-use shopping precinct, combined with high-end residential development and hotels. The latest high-profile addition to the precinct is a grain silo conversion by London-based Heatherwick Studio, which includes a luxury hotel and the location for the future Zeitz Museum of Contemporary Art Africa (MOCAA), which opened in late 2017. The second site occupation is in Woodstock, a vacant hospital in close proximity to the galleries, restaurants and design quarter that define the neighbourhood's gentrification.

The choice of sites is not only strategic, but also indicative of the value of focusing light on the spatial paradoxes that have come to define Cape Town. This is evident in the choice of infographics and mapping shared on social media, the visual depiction of glamour of the city in contradiction to the hardships of those on the edges, and the personal stories. More recently, the focus has been on Airbnb's expansion into the city and the location of short-term rentals. Here, the appropriation of the capacity of data is most obvious, as online maps illustrate the impact on land and property markets. This part of the campaign never reached the extents of protest against accommodation platforms elsewhere (Cocola-Gant and Gago, 2019; van Doorn, 2019). The visual representation of the extent to which the majority of Capetonians are unable to afford well-located housing did strike a chord, however. The city and provincial governments have since formulated inclusionary housing policies that acknowledge the skewed nature of the city's property market.

In addition to the spikes in activity that identified the milestones and entry points of connection to the campaign, the various actors engaged in an ongoing mobilization process that formed a 'slow burn' of diverse activities. The most significant, politically, was the legal campaign to stop the sale of the Tafelberg site, as mentioned earlier. Later, there was an online and offline campaign to object to zoning proposals for the Somerset Precinct near the Waterfront (containing the property that was occupied by activists) to allow for more social housing. The latter is indicative of the contest of numbers that played itself out as occupancy ratios and floor space allocations were debated. Selective representation of data is evident in both camps, however! RtC is as astute as the City of Cape Town in ensuring that the numbers 'dance' in ways that support their arguments.

A significant part of the campaign was to raise the consciousness of the public. This includes information sharing in public spaces, regular editorial content by activists and supporters, and targeted alliances with stakeholder groups, such as the Sea Point Jewish Community (an established interest group in the neighbourhood), other state agencies and property development interest groups. As an alternative to the usual economic discourse that favours an unfettered property market, the message that well-located social housing makes economic sense for households and the city represents a significant shift in the public consciousness. This was later reflected in an inner-city housing plan launched in July 2017 that designated a number of well-located sites within the city core for social housing. More recently, in 2021, the provincial government launched its own inclusionary housing policy.

While the RtC campaign cannot be portrayed as a model for smart city appropriation (I would argue that no such thing exists) and a deeper interrogation will no doubt reveal some inconsistencies and inaccuracies, it nevertheless represents an impressive intervention that has achieved a significant shift in public awareness in its short time span. The scaffoldings of its organizational structure and its activism reveal an array of online and offline strategies that range from a populist representation of information to a technically astute interrogation of commonplace 'truths' regarding property markets and the space economy of the city. A significant part of the campaign is the foregrounding of the 'everyday' experiences of city dwellers in the face of gentrification and, some would argue, state inaction. The enrolment of emotional, technical and political 'stories' into the campaign's narrative, together with the ongoing labour of legal, media and policy engagement, represents a fascinating entry point into what cyborg activism may look like and what its potential is for effecting change.

NU and CTT: platform strategies for community mobilization

I reconnected with NU[4] and members of CTT at the time of writing to probe the specifics of the use of digital platforms in more detail. After the success of the RtC campaign, NU has embarked on other initiatives that address spatial exclusion and has become a significant feature of the city's civil society landscape. Some of this included a collaboration with CTT on campaigning for the release of other parcels of publicly owned land for social housing. I was particularly curious as to the combination of the different functionalities of platform elements in the organizations' mobilization strategies. Here, I find the notion of 'cyborg activism' particularly compelling. It speaks to a hybridity that recurs throughout this book. The 'cyborg' motif, as an entity that integrates and transcends the visceral boundaries of the body shaped by biology, provides a useful frame for understanding data-mediated activism. The intimate exchange between algorithm, human and urban space entails a reassembling of the individual as containing elements of human and machine, or nature and technology (Asenbaum, 2018). In thinking through the elements of a technology-mediated activism, the usual 'binaries' of nature versus technology, identity versus anonymity and public versus private are reconfigured to allow for the reason–emotion divide to blur (Asenbaum, 2018).

Kyla Hazell, Popular Education Officer, and Michael Clark, the Head of Research and Advocacy, both at NU, referred to the Tafelberg case often in our discussion on how traditional and new media were strategically combined to not only inform the public, but also gather support. During the proceedings, daily protest vigils were hosted outside the court building, hard-copy pamphlets were distributed and press releases were updated daily in media summaries to journalists, with live tweeting throughout the process. Tweets were shared to WhatsApp groups. These live summaries increased engagement and interaction. Shifting popular opinion was a conscious aim throughout the process.[5] Capturing the public imagination and empowering organizers to gain insight into the legal frameworks that inform spatial planning and housing were also enabled through on-site theatre, online video and cartoons on social media. This is, then, where the storytelling aspect features. Capturing people's everyday realities and stories is an important aspect of the organization's work, with the use of video having become particularly poignant. Furthermore, making information digestible and accessible using new media is a feature of using Instagram for infographics, for example, capturing the essence of an argument in a visually stimulating and interesting way.[6]

An example is a current campaign (at the time of writing) aimed at the release of unused or underutilized publicly owned land for inclusionary housing. Social media posts preceded a virtual public meeting that was held on 8 June 2021. What is evident in the Instagram pictorial, as well as the Facebook posts, is a combination of technical and popular communication skills. Mapping is combined with technical projections, quantified facts and campaign information on future action. The 'slides' on Instagram (see Figure 5.1) contribute to an arc, or a storyboard, culminating in a conclusion that emphasizes the importance for release of state-owned vacant land for

Figure 5.1: Ndifuna Ukwazi vacant land release campaign on Instagram

Source: NU's Instagram account (available at: @ndifunaukwazi)

affordable housing. It is aimed at broadening support for the campaign by extolling values that would have a broad appeal and structuring overarching messages that the public can identify with by humanizing the message through examples that the general public can relate to.

Numeric evidence and visual representation are combined to elicit minds and hearts,[7] 'enabling nodes around which relationships form and alliances are built. ... Within networks, narrative technologies allow new relationships with other actors', as Kellogg's (2016: 44) work on the Cuban blog Voces Cubanas suggests. The aesthetic differs from the usual soft Instagram pastel imagery, with the use of bold colours, capital letters and challenging imagery. This was a conscious choice to depart from the usual Instagram visual language, intentionally causing some discomfort, raising awareness through engagement, and evoking an emotional response to posts.[8] By appealing to people's sensibilities as to what is considered 'decent' and using data discerningly, NU creates nodes of interest that enrol combinations of stakeholders not usually in agreement. In a city as divided as Cape Town, this is very poignant. According to Hazell, the use of Instagram opens up space for this unexpected engagement, where careful thought is put into how to 'land a message', while preserving an accurate digital archive.[9] The capturing of a digital archive, in combination with the facts that drive the campaign, is something that is critical to NU's communication campaign.

In discussion with NU and CTT, mention was made of how campaigning is also influenced by platform market trends. The interoperability between Facebook and Instagram enables the integration of campaign messages and expansion of audiences. Facebook is used for visual media, with the commenting particularly useful for understanding oppositional stances (through trolls, for example) and for gauging the public imagination in general. Facebook is a space to engage specific audiences with evidence and to determine impacts.[10] Its free data function is also more enabling.

The danger of troll action undermining the efficacy of Facebook sites is nevertheless acknowledged by CTT and NU. For the CTT CANs, it was essential to use the organization's 'ways of working' mandate to inform the parameters of communication, with a dedicated team of moderators keeping an eye. Both organizations stressed the importance of storytelling within bounds, with moderators 'holding the space' in relation to the CANs given the open-endedness of the networks' actions.[11]

WhatsApp is the platform reported as most useful and effective in the activities of CANs and NU. As a bounded system of groups and broadcasts, as well as having sharing and editing functions, there is enough guarantee of privacy yet a growing capacity to expand networks. NU uses WhatsApp for sharing information and press briefings in pre-selected journalist groups. The interoperability and internal architecture of the platform allows for social connection in a controlled fashion. The editing functions enable messaging to be personalized. According to Brady, the CTT template for sharing and associated values captured in the 'ways of working' mandate also helped build trust on WhatsApp. Interestingly, NU summarized Twitter feeds on WhatsApp for its organizers, as well as daily court proceedings during the Tafelberg hearing. Twitter does play a role, though not extensively. It is useful for responding to public figures in 'real time' and to stay current. However, it is largely seen as an 'elitist' online space,[12] used in very specific ways by NU staff and not by CTT as part of its main operations.

The class dynamic is evident is what remains a stubborn 'digital divide', with the cost of data and smartphones an issue, particularly with CANs in poorer neighbourhoods. People use media in relation to their demographic profile, the purpose of interaction and in terms of levels of trust. The tone of exchanges is also informed by the choice of medium: 'As the private pervades public spaces, the modern separation of *rationality*, objectivity and cool-headed politics, on one hand, and *emotion*, passion and affect, on the other, is reconfigured' (Asenbaum, 2018: 5, emphasis in original). NU respondents referred to the irreverence that the organization has come to be known for as a feature of platform-enabled communication. The cheekiness of some of the posts and the courage to speak to political power with confidence, backed up by evidence, is most certainly enabled through new media. This was seen to be part of the identity of NU.

Whereas the values and notions of acting 'at the speed of trust' by CANs was also seen as a departure from traditional organizing, enabled through a range of technologies in combination with other forms of media such as radio and print media, the sway of the 'slow burn' of ongoing networking and mobilization builds alternative narratives. Using a socio-technical lens in his work on Cuba, Kellogg (2016: 33) writes of the heterogeneous range of actors that contribute to networks becoming 'cyborg entities, homeostatic assemblages of heterogeneous techno-social elements with porous borders and radical political motivations'. In his research, the written narrative, produced in blog form, is an actant that contains flexibility and fluidity, potentially shaping political discourse. In the cases of NU and CTT, discourses evolve in relation to a predetermined set of values and intentions, part of which is significantly informed by local contexts. The legacy of intergenerational struggle is a strong element in both examples of mobilization. The lessons and methods of established activists were acknowledged by all three respondents, but the urban context brings with it a more youthful and irreverent sensibility, enhanced through new media. The latter affords greater opportunities for adaptability and quick responses to crises.

The importance of place is central to the activities of RtC and NU due to the spatial focus of the campaign itself, as well as the stories that relate so specifically to home and identity. Media and social online platforms use photo essays and personal stories to shine a light on household struggles, while the networking capacity of social media is used to thematically connect disparate accounts into an overall narrative that challenges the market logics of property speculation. The networking capacity of new media is also employed in the creation of a hashtag portal – an online 'place' where diverse voices can be collated around particular moments or events in the campaign. Creating 'collective sense-making spaces'[13] is a function of the relational space created by cyborg activism.

In summary, combining the evidence specific to place and cause while engaging the public at large, in styles appropriate to organizational values, is perhaps the most overt manifestation of platform-enhanced activism. There are nevertheless a number of risks for CSOs. There is the danger of oversimplifying the message, with a fine line negotiated between accuracy and accessibility.[14] Personal safety is a risk due to the public exposure afforded by social media, making certain groups very vulnerable to harassment. NU has also experienced cybersecurity issues. Losing nuance is seen as a big issue. Furthermore, the public is often unaware of the work and research that supports online activism, reading the content on social media one-dimensionally. Despite these constraints and risks, the reframing of evidence and thereby regeneration of knowledge around and about the city are forms of social mobilization that are relational and contingent. The next section explores this further.

Knowledge generation as activism

At a meeting at the World Urban Forum in Medellín, Colombia, in 2014, I found myself in the company of geographic information system (GIS) specialists advocating a 'smart city from the bottom up', unusual language for this world, in my experience. The presentation was part of the SDI's 'Know Your City' campaign, supported by United Cities and Local Governments of Africa (UCLG-A) and the Cities Alliance. As an academic that engages spatial relationships and attaches them to human experience, I found this to be an interesting prospect. Documenting the facts and figures of the 'shadow cities'[15] comprising informal settlements is essential to informing a public response that is based on local experiences. As part of the campaign, communities drive data-gathering processes, generating concrete information that they own and manage. This work creates alternative systems of knowledge that are owned by the slum communities. The SDI resources speak to the potential for forming collaborative partnerships in the collection, verification and storage of data, or, more specifically, slum profiling.

The roles of technology in achieving the aims of the campaign relate to facilitating contact between residents and authorities, disseminating information, being used as a reporting tool and collecting crowdsourced data. It also gets highlighted a number of times as a means to mobilize and enhance capacities to keep local government accountable.[16] A further function listed is data triangulation by using data sources from a variety of stakeholders that are available on a range of media platforms.

SDI is a network with local affiliates across the Global South. One of its collaborators, working with affiliates in West Africa, is the SLURC. The SLURC was established in 2016, supported by the Bartlett University College London (UCL) Development Planning Unit (DPU) and the Institute of Geography and Development Studies at Njala University, and funded by Comic Relief.[17] The aim of establishing the institution was to build the local research capacity of local professionals and communities, and to determine a contextually appropriate research agenda (Rigon et al, 2017). A further aim was to enable partnerships with local urban actors and local SDI affiliates. Thus, the framing of a research agenda, together with local actors, was crucial to setting it up.

The SLURC has established itself as a mediating platform that works with slum communities, local governments and local CSOs. An example cited is where research on livelihoods in informal settlements incorporated the SLURC, DPU, the Federation of the Urban Poor (FEDUP), local SDI affiliates and the Pul Slum Pan People (PSPP) network, which is active in Freetown's informal settlements (Rigon et al, 2017). I thought it appropriate to use the SLURC as an entry point to examine how digital platforms contribute to, and enable, a knowledge-generation project that essentially sees data collection as a form of collective action. In a general meeting with stakeholders in Freetown, representatives stressed the need to go beyond the use of books, journals and other publications to generate knowledge, and to use a podcast, blogs, the radio and online resources to disseminate data (Daramy, 2021). What frames this approach is an organizational commitment to participatory action research,[18] which was well displayed in the response to COVID-19 lockdown measures in 2020.

The flow of data from the community to the SLURC was effectively digitized when COVID-19 led to shutdowns. The use of mobile phones and video was an essential part of staying in touch with slum communities. Together with FEDUP, media specialists within the community were trained to make short videos for incidence reporting. The SLURC would then edit and disseminate. These recorded experiences inform the community area action plans being prepared by the SLURC and local communities. They are also available on the Centre of Dialogue on Human Settlement and Poverty Alleviation's (CODOHSAPA's) and FEDUP's web sites as the 'Know Your City' TV channel. Using such perspectives captures the experiential dimensions of life in informal settlements.

The WhatsApp platform is again cited as the most useful app for disseminating information to interest groups and officials. Reference was made to the use of the app to enable mapping of *okada* routes (the West African version of *boda-bodas*) in order to analyse the spatial distribution of routes and how paratransit fits with other modes. Fieldworkers also work together with slum dwellers in using Ramblr[19] to map informal areas for community action area plans.[20] All these methods and applications are used as needed but clearly provide the means whereby stakeholder groups and state actors can be enrolled into networks of communication and information dissemination. The legitimacy of such networks is, to some extent, enhanced through the location of the SLURC as a research body, as well as a policy influencer. The capture of data and putting slum communities on the map, together with the recording of stories that convey the experiential aspects of infrastructure failure and the impact of COVID-19, are enabled through a range of technologies. The use of video, in particular, makes the invisible 'visible', using the SDI's language for the 'Know Your City' campaign.

The use of digital media to gather data is, of course, meaningful, but how those data are represented to the state (in cases where the SLURC and partners aim at influencing debates) and harnessed towards shaping public opinion (in the case of NU) or to enhance neighbourhood networks often results in visual representation that is immediately legible and digestible. Data are represented in thoughtful and intentional ways to deliver a particular message. In the following section, the data speaks for themselves.

Elevated perspectives

> 'We live within neighborhoods and participate in economies that reinforce inequality. We habituate ourselves with routines and take for granted the built environment of our cities. We're shocked seeing tin shacks and dilapidated buildings hemmed into neat rows, bounded by the fences, roads, and parks of the wealthiest few.
>
> But it's the very scale and unerring regularity across geographic regions which points to the systemic nature of inequality. This is not organic – this is planned and intentional disenfranchisement.'
> (Johnny Miller[21])

Seeing the scale at which inequality manifests is a large part of what drone photography can achieve. Changing perspectives on our experiences of cities is sometimes best achieved by moving outside our comfort zones – in some cases, taking an elevated perspective. Johnny Miller has used drone photography to illustrate these contrasts at scale. He has done this all over the world, but more particularly, his work on South African cities has received particular commendation, appearing, for example, on the cover of *Time* magazine and, more recently, in *The Economist*.

'Unequal Scenes' has won a number of international awards, and exhibitions have been hosted at the World Urban Forum in 2020 and the Lagos Photo Festival, among many others. The drone photography is used to tell stories, and on Miller's 'Unequal Scenes' web site,[22] he takes it a

Figure 5.2: Lake Michelle and Masiphumelele, Cape Town

Source: Photograph by Johnny Miller (available at: https://unequalscenes.com/south-africa)

step further by formulating 'An action guide on reducing inequality'. The drone photography is combined with infographics to deliver a poignant message intended to inspire action, providing links to initiatives that can be pursued further by the reader, such as the UN Global Compact Action Guide and The Narrative Initiative. A telling phrase in the document is: 'Every moment is fundamentally underpinned by "ordinary people".'[23]

Miller is a founding member of African Drone, an organization that seeks to empower drone pilots through training and technical assistance, as well as to promote the use of drones 'for good' on the continent.[24] Set up as an African-led team of drone pilots, tech enthusiasts and journalists, as well as regulators, the aim is also to enable a 'Better understanding of the world around us, using drone technology.'[25] Some of this requires assistance with navigating regulations for flying drones, connecting drone pilots with content creators and enabling direct commissions. Africa Drone is a key participant in the Lake Victoria Challenge, last held in Tanzania in 2018, with the intention of promoting drone technology as a form of mobility and delivery. The emphasis is on training and innovation. Much of this is reliant on a regulatory environment that ensures safety yet also allows for experimentation – a difficult balance to achieve and a tricky terrain to negotiate should it not exist. This is a recurrent theme in this book.

Conclusion

The generation of knowledge using digital tools is an immensely visual exercise, as is evident in all the vignettes under discussion. However, creating an alternative discourse to data-mediated policy perspectives and official narratives requires ongoing social action to shift narratives in order to focus attention on systemic issues. Dissensus provides one such window onto systemic inequality (Kaika, 2017). Understanding the scaffoldings of such dissensus, that is, the means through which it is communicated and represented, provides insight into strategies of knowledge production that takes us to a more accurate representation of smart urbanism. It necessitates technology appropriation, but it also implies an aspirational shifting of policy discourses. Furthermore, I would argue, it entails conveying an experiential dimension to sharing that seeks to evoke an emotional response. In this chapter, I have explored four different forms of knowledge sharing and co-production through the use of platforms. NU and the CTT network of CANs are both based in Cape Town, are drawn to similar issues of exclusion and poverty, and have collaborated but do differ slightly in their strategies. NU directly confronts the state, reminds it of its mandate and challenges its policies. In doing so, the organization uses a suite of digital and analogue tools to inform and mobilize. CTT responded to the pandemic by providing a frame for self-organizing networks at the neighbourhood scale. This has caused some friction in dealing with authorities that take a more centralized and controlled approach to public health management. Both organizations shared important reflections on the suite of platforms used and their roles. The emphasis on respecting and acknowledging experiential knowledge is foregrounded in both these examples.

Dramatic portrayals of 'everyday' suffering tap into the public imagination. NU and CTT see this as central to their mandates. Work elsewhere shows some visceral evidence, such as Robins' (2014b) work on the 'poo-protests' in Cape Town, where (among other public actions) activists emptied human waste onto the concourse of the Cape Town International Airport to draw attention to the adverse sanitation conditions in informal settlements on the city's fringes. Here, information was transmitted through visual media, hashtagging in order to link events in real time and draw the attention of the mainstream media. The power of the spectacle lies in elevating issues to policy discourses: 'Prior to the Toilet Wars, the shocking sanitation conditions in informal settlements seldom made it into the mainstream media or national political discourse' (Robins, 2014b: 480). In this chapter, I have aimed to show how digital strategies fit into the hybrid range of mobilization tools, some of which are deployed as spectacle.

The discussion has revealed how context informs the interplay between digital and analogue, saying much about activist aims, the profile of participants and the nature of the problem being addressed. In fact, it reveals a lot about the textures of platform urbanism.

Besides the drama of the oft-used spectacle, there is also the 'slow burn' that is necessary for meaningful change, that is, the 'bricolage' that connects people and technology to exert pressure on the state through the usual means of protest marches, press releases, judiciary action and so on. The NU example, in particular, shows a finely grained and continuous exchange between online and offline spaces in a form of cyborg activism that is deeply relational. Importantly, the work that enables knowledge networks sustains an ongoing discursive alternative to that which the state represents. That work, the 'slow activism' that Robins (2014a) refers to, builds on alliances stretched over time and across geographic boundaries, as well as political economies. In South Africa, relationships forged during anti-apartheid activism now manifest in new forms. Much of this is enabled through a free press and a context that allows for civil society activism. Where such organizing is not possible without repercussions, the ability of digital media to enable network relations across time–space geographies is meaningful.

The work that technology does, in concert with human agency, forms part of alliance building and network making. In not only the Cuban example explored by Kellogg, but also Robins' work on South Africa, it challenges the state's control of knowledge, being productive of 'alternative discursive spaces and subversive narratives' (Kellogg, 2016: 23). It is performative and experiential. The power of the spectacle is that it evokes an emotional response that lingers in the public imagination and carries political currency. Combining it with the 'slow burn' is powerful and yields results, as we see in Cape Town. The use of spectacle is therefore not only a media strategy to shine a dramatic light on injustice, but also a means to create 'choreographies of assembly' that, together with devices like hashtags, become trending places and magnetic, heterogeneous assemblages (Gerbaudo, 2012: 12). The emotional tension created through social media acts as a different kind of aggregator from numeric means, constructing common symbols and momentary unified identities from diverse participants, or what the activist Zackie Achmat, in Robins' (2014a) portrayal of the Social Justice Coalition in Cape Town, refers to as a 'moral consensus'.

Thus, a recurrent theme is how platforms enable elasticity across scales and between the social and the personal. The experiential dimension becomes a key part of data gathering and representation, from slum settlements in Freetown, to gentrified neighbourhoods in Cape Town. Thus, the experiential dimension is key to not only mobilizing consensus and assembly, but also creating a data of dissension that combines the 'slow burn' of monitoring, reporting and information processing, with emotionally charged representations of suffering. In appropriating technology, its emergent qualities are enrolled as time and situation demand. Kyla Hazell, from NU, shared a telling personal dimension as to how these hybrid forms of activism capture one's own imagination of what is possible. The question is: are these largely fleeting assemblies situationally focused, or do they represent epistemological and ontological shifts, where the experiential and emotional dimensions or urban data can shift public discourse, or, essentially, what counts as knowledge and truth? It is clear that this is not a passing fad; all the vignettes share a shift in mobilization techniques that embraces the personal as political. It is to this theme that I now turn: how these forms of cyborg activism and general platform engagement contribute to revised notions of the public, and what to make of these reformed imaginaries.

6

Platform Practices and the Public Imagination

Introduction

In an interview in *Chimurenga* magazine, provocatively entitled 'The Internet is Afropolitan', Achille Mbembe is quoted as saying: 'Technology is nothing without the capacity to make people dream. That is where the power of technology resides.'[1] I believe that the imagination that is vested in the power of technology carries with it a re-imagining of urban futures. Clues as to how this future is actively re-imagined in urban practices can be found in the vignettes captured in this book. Throughout the three themes preceding this chapter, the interface between local cultures and technology appropriation has been largely implicit, though central to the overall theoretical trajectory of this book.

In their book on *The Public and Their Platforms*, Carrigan and Fatsis (2021) write of the tendency of platforms to disassociate from place, predominantly through the sidestepping of local regulatory environments, Uber being a prime example. The experiences documented in this book suggest otherwise. In the discussion of SafeBoda in Chapter 3, for example, the influence of the cultural and regulatory environment influences the introduction of the app in different country contexts. Regulatory frameworks do impact on how platform urbanism lands, but they are not always documented or enshrined in legislation. Such frameworks can be negotiable, as in the *boda-boda* industry in Uganda, for example, where operational parameters are a continuous source of debate.

There are more subtle dynamics at work that relate to localized notions of public and private, as well as the more experiential informants of place. Beyond regulation and urban planning guidelines are the 'ways of doing' and local forms of being in the city that inform place and elements associated with its making. The remediation of public life through digital exchange, the sharing of experiences and information across scales, and the hybrid nature of the socio-technical networks that underpin these experiences all contribute to a reframing of the public (Odendaal, 2021b).

This final thematic chapter explores the notion of the public in more detail, exploring several dimensions that inform this, such as some of the dynamics that are specific to African urban spaces that impact public culture and place, in order to understand the less overt, yet ingrained, qualities that influence the appropriation of technology in particular contexts. In doing this, I explore the concepts of the public and place by examining three place-based expressions of technology in place: MapKibera, innovation hubs and GoDown (an arts centre in Nairobi). While all three are in Kenya, the latter two examples are complimentary: hubs are incubators for technology workers and GoDown is a hub for artists that extend into the digital realm. Furthermore, the latter is also an extension into the city, aiming at marrying public space with the arts, and vice versa.

What emerges from the chapters thus far is this hybrid nature of the disrupted city, where digital and analogue lives are intertwined, and where the 'old' and 'new' reinforce each other in an ongoing dance of socio-technical evolution. The aim here is to examine what it is about the old and new that reflects a particular cultural disposition towards technology. What is the imagination that drives the use and appropriation of technological artefacts, and the incorporation of them into urban African lifestyles? Here, MapKibera is significant as an example of mapping publics and engaging them across platforms, making sense of place and thereby claiming its place on the map.

It is therefore fitting to spend the latter part of this chapter on how the digital imagination manifests in interpretations of the future of cities on the continent. Here, the journey takes us back to West Africa, though curiously also to the US by including Afro-diasporic interpretations of future African cities, capturing the collective imagination of technology and urban futures by exploring Afrofuturism. Here, the examination of cultural practices intends to uncover what imagined futures may be. In his PhD thesis, Baumann (2018) gives an account of the Sankofa Project, a collaborative project in Los Angeles in which he was a key actor, where disruptive technologies were incorporated into the making of place in a way that reflected local social norms and aesthetic values. In doing so, he recounts the inspiration afforded by Afrofuturism in stoking the imagination of possible futures.

Womack (2013: 191) speaks of how the collection of theory and literature that inspires social change called 'Afrofuturism' does the following:

> Afrofuturism is a great tool for wielding the imagination for personal change and societal growth. Empowering people to see themselves and their ideas in the future gives rise to innovators and free thinkers, all

of whom can pull from the best of the past while navigating the sea of possibilities to create communities, culture, and a new, balanced world.

I believe a key part of this work in relation to considering the future of digitally enhanced African cities is expanding on the relationship between socio-technical change, the notion of the public, public culture, the present qualities of place and imaginations of possible futures. This requires a conceptual framing that is informed by the preceding three chapters and the literature on Afrofuturism. In many ways, this chapter is the bridge between the present and future, as well as the final foray into the real and imagined worlds of the African smart city before I consider the implications in Chapter 7.

On (re)claiming the public sphere and embracing citizenship in the everyday

In a book by Carrigan and Fatsis (2021), entitled *The Public and Their Platforms*, the authors explore the notion of the public very eloquently; they are particularly interested in how the notion of the public has changed due to COVID-19 and the reliance on digital platforms. Part of this project is a redefinition of the term 'public', which is outlined as: 'an ecosystem or an associational infrastructure which is composed of a sense of self (identity) and a way of life (practice) that makes room (space) for citizenship in everyday life' (Carrigan and Fatsis, 2021: 28).

During the COVID-19 pandemic, we have come to rely on digital platforms for social interaction. The authors explore the ways in which the merging of the digital and the analogue has impacted public life, more specifically, and particularly pertinent to the theme of this book, the ways through which digital platforms have impacted on how we define public life in a broader urban setting.

The discussions with respondents engaged in social mobilization in Cape Town in Chapter 5, together with consideration of the aims of SafeBoda in Chapter 3 and the intricacies of ensuring local food security in Chapter 4, foreground the associational networks that enable livelihoods for many. Whether it concerns *boda-boda* riders in Kampala, *mama mbongas* in Nairobi or street activists in Cape Town, localized kinship networks are critical. During the COVID-19 pandemic, they essentially formed part of an 'infrastructure of care' in South African cities (Odendaal, 2021a), where the distribution of food and medical assistance during lockdown was largely enabled through online and offline networks. The term 'associational life' became popular in academic literature in relation to the African context in the early 2000s, largely informed by concerns around weak government and infrastructure breakdown.

Defining associational life relates to how civil society is conceptualized in relation to larger governance processes. The use of social media and digital applications is informed, to some extent, by press freedom, for example, and regulatory frameworks that relate to the specifics of the issues under contestation. If one is to define the public as an arena of exchange between actors representing divergent interests, then the role of the state becomes critical to understanding the nature of popular mobilization. Does the state allow for freedom of expression, for example? Do regulations restrict popular protest? And how does the state relate to the informal? In the three preceding chapters, the state features as an antagonistic attempted regulator of the paratransit industry, an inadvertent undermining force in food distribution during the COVID-19 pandemic and an opponent to inclusionary housing. Sometimes, the state can be a partner, a neutral bystander or enabler in relation to civil society organization (Tostensen et al, 2001). Associational life features in social mobilization and the many textures of the everyday. With social media and platform technology, the social is broadened and the everyday exists in several experiential dimensions. These networks expand from place and across space, deepening the sense of public self relationally.

Thus, a reconsideration of how the public is re-imagined is critical to understanding notions of citizenship in relation to platform urbanism. The reinvention of public space and the repurposing of places through digital application speaks to renewed platforms for citizenship, influenced by the sensibilities and activities that take place in them (Carrigan and Fatsis, 2021). In this section, I focus specifically on a set of urban practices that engage place, public space and the broader public realm, examined from a number of angles. The first subsection contains an explicit endeavour to map space and the network publics that emerge from that process. The second subsection examines the notion of innovation hubs as spaces intended to foster connection and innovation, but that are impacted by global discourses and knowledge networks. The third subsection examines the use of artists' practices to network and engage, and how and where platforms feature in this process.

MapKibera

Much has been written about MapKibera, or, indeed, about Kibera in general, given its status as one of the largest slums in Africa. That does not undermine how remarkable the initiative is. In Chapter 5, I used the phrase 'making the invisible "visible"' as a summarized explanation of the importance of data capture and knowledge generation in informal areas. This is, in fact, the strapline used by MapKibera on its web site, as well as by the SDI 'Know Your City' campaign. This aspiration clearly resonates! The work with the SLURC shows that there is a tendency for governments to designate the informal as illegal or illegitimate – 'blank' spaces that are either left well alone or, worse, eradicated. The work of the SLURC and SDI in relation to the Know Your City campaign is to lend legitimacy to these spaces through data capture and knowledge production. In Kibera, this 'blank space' comprises 2.5 km² of urban life, sorted into 13 villages with over 200,000 residents.[2]

The MapKibera project, led by Erika Hagen and Mikel Maron, initially trained carefully selected and representative residents from Kibera in using a range of technologies to map and collect stories about local places in the area, resulting in dense maps capturing points of interest, categorized and selected by participants (Hagen, 2010). Java editing software was used to map and share these data through OpenStreetMap, a community-driven 'Wikipedia of maps' that captures local knowledge about places. The project has evolved into three spinoffs that illustrate the generative potential of such work. With support from funding partners, more detailed mapping on prioritized thematic areas has been done, which includes ongoing media development using tools made by Ushahidi (an East African non-profit company that develops open-source software) that enable mapping through the use of mobile phones, online video news reporting and SMS monitoring of local issues (Hagen, 2010). The result is the Kibera News Network on YouTube and Voice of Kibera radio (Hagen, 2017). This learning is now used in two other slums in Nairobi, and the web site has evolved into a training platform where information and techniques are shared.

My last visit to Kibera was after the National Kenyan elections in 2017. A large part of the discussion with MapKibera staff evolved around the security issues during the election, associated violence and the spread of misinformation.[3] The three dimensions of the MapKibera Trust's work were discussed: first, citizen mapping of crime hot spots (specifically with the input of young girls and women), clinics and hospitals, polling stations, police points, safe places, and so on; second, citizen media through SMS reporting at polling stations and video; and, third, citizen advocacy, specifically focused on debunking misinformation through the use of radio and video.

In a recent report, Erika Hagen (2017), the co-founder of the MapKibera Trust, provides a very thorough reflection on the evolution of the trust over its first ten years. In probing the relationship between technology application, local community transparency and social accountability, I found her reflections on the actual processes of map making particularly poignant. The process was very respectful of local knowledge and priorities: 'We taught them *how* to map, but not *what* to map' (Hagen, 2017: 6, emphases in original). Thus, inhabitants initially mapped what they considered important to make visible to the community. Furthermore, meetings with community members were used to verify the information and representation on the maps. Hagen reflects on the tendency of NGOs and development agencies to collect data within Kibera but generally share it outside the area (to donors, academic partners and so on). Addressing this by equalizing 'the information

Figure 6.1: Kibera security map in situ

Source: Photograph by author

asymmetry' was seen as critical. This certainly resonates with the trends elsewhere, as discussed in relation to the SLURC and SDI in Chapter 5.

There is, however, a particular dynamic in relation to the notion of the public, that I would like to explore further. A mix of media is used in consulting stakeholders through mapping. Paper maps were used in conjunction with digital representation and distributed accordingly. Hagen (2017) makes a telling comment based on her research about the wall map depicted in Figure 6.1: such maps were used by residents as general maps of the area and provided an awareness of MapKibera and its activities, but they were not necessarily used as tools of advocacy. This is no small thing, I would argue. The development of a spatial literacy that stretches across media and scales, and relating that back to places that matter, is a form of empowerment and connection to place. It is a form of subtle activism that reasserts awareness of the public, or of place, through online and offline mapping. Putting a field, a place of danger to young women, a security point and unsafe tracks on a map reaffirms that they exist. It also becomes part of the sense making of place.

There are figurative and literal technology spaces. Hagen (2017: 24) found that, when asked, MapKibera participants were comfortable with technology and around technology, for example, in Nairobi's iHub. There was most definitely a sense of ownership and pride when I visited the MapKibera Trust's office in 2018. The modest project office was hard to find in among the tuck shops and shacks, but once inside, it was evident that this was an important place of information capture and dissemination. In what Hagen (2017: 24) refers to as 'process-related' empowerment, her respondents displayed a departure from any social norms that tech is the domain of only the university-educated elite. Not only are they known for being tech savvy, but they are trusted and seen as reliable sources of local information and mapping. Building trust networks through an open community data process created the conditions for substantive investments in, for example, local schools and security points. In my own discussion with staff, there was particular emphasis made on the value of offline and online work, and the distribution of public information across a range of media.

As Hagen (2017: 30) notes in her report, the processes of data collection could potentially create more impactful systemic change: 'participating in the process of becoming visible on one's own terms helps generate the type of trust which can lead to connections within the larger network of actors'. The platforms used and expanded upon by the trust's staff may have initially emphasized ensuring the documentation of landmarks or places of importance for residents, but it is the expansion that it enabled that put Kibera on the map, as a place, a home and a public.

Technology hubs

In many of the interactions that I have had about the intensification of digital economic and social exchanges, a bemused local view is taken of the notion of the 'Silicon Savannah', a term often used to refer to the update of the platform economy in East Africa. Indeed, all the examples I look at in this subsection are in Nairobi, what many in the corporate sector see as the regional centre for the creative class and the knowledge economy (Rosenberg and Brent, 2020). The growth of the number of ICT hubs in Kenya, and Nairobi in particular, has added to the platform gloss, informed by policy language that tends to be technologically determinist. The city's strategic plan, 'Nairobi Metro 2030', as well as the country's development plan, entitled 'Vision 2030', sees ICT as a driver of economic growth, with an emphasis on the provision of infrastructure for technology services, as well as the inevitable smart city programme. The most notable is Konza Tech City, another source of mirth in my discussions with Kenyan colleagues and friends. Local scholars question the technocentric, top-down approach taken in engendering a knowledge economy (Guma and Monstadt, 2020) and the lack of understanding of livelihood strategies impacted by these policies. In some ways, innovation hubs in the city are seen as counter to decentralized satellite cities, such as Konza Tech City. The hype surrounding the iHub and other tech hubs in Nairobi given press and academic attention (Afrilabs and Briter-Bridges, 2019; Friederici, 2018; Jiménez and Zheng, 2021) is worthy of discussion due to their proliferation as places of connection and incubation, essentially, networking spaces for the growing tech entrepreneurial class.

It is perhaps best to start with the definitions and stated intentions of digital innovation hubs. They are physical places – often with a couple of desks, some whiteboards, good Wi-Fi and a social space – which provide nodes for technology workers. There are several characteristics of hubs that speak to an interesting dynamic between aspirations and implementation (Friederici, 2018; Toivonen and Friederici, 2015). An aspiration for building community, using a physical space to enable collaboration and networking is a feature of the popular literature on hubs. Yet, they also rely on self-motivated individual agency for ensuring that the group dynamic of hubs thrive (Toivonen and Friederici, 2015). A friendly tension exists between embracing individual agency and valuing the potential for co-creation and collaboration. The emphasis on heterogeneity, where a range of skills and backgrounds is encouraged, is thought to encourage innovation and 'out of the box' thinking. Yet, a 'go-getter' attitude of innovative leadership is also expected, or, at least, there is an expectation of expansion beyond the physical space of the hub.

An associated dynamic that I believe is integral to understanding the notion of public in relation to the platform economy is the relationship between local places and global spaces. By 2019, over 600 hubs had been identified in Africa, including tech incubators, accelerators and hybrid innovation spaces shared with universities, governments and corporates. Only 25 per cent of these offer support beyond a physical place with basic infrastructure (Afrilabs and Briter-Bridges, 2019). The security and companionship offered by a physical place feature as important characteristics of hubs; they are seen as safe spaces for young innovators, rather than venture builders (Afrilabs and Briter-Bridges, 2019). As co-working spaces, hubs offer respite from infrastructure (especially electricity) interruption, relatively fast and stable Wi-Fi, and opportunities for connection (Rosenberg and Brent, 2020).

Hubs are funded by membership fees, donor funding and consulting. According to Afrilabs and Briter-Bridges (2019), 60 per cent of funding is received from donors, including corporate sponsors, NGOs and philanthropic organizations. Many use affiliations with corporates to fund cloud storage, servers, fibre-optic cables and other forms of digital infrastructure (Afrilabs and Briter-Bridges, 2019). Evidence across Africa does indicate an increase in the density and extent of international networking (Afrilabs and Briter-Bridges, 2019), but the dependence on foreign donors for funding is unsustainable.

The contrast between user experiences and the discursive strategies that drive the proliferation of hubs often relates to global ideals. Tech hubs are increasingly relied on for economic and employment impact that is often beyond their scope, with the emphasis more recently on post-COVID-19 recovery,[4] as reflected in Kenya's 'Vision 2030'. The 'network infrastructure expectation', as Friederici (2018) puts it, sees hubs as part of a web of global connections that includes important global partners, connecting tech entrepreneurs across the continent. How effective these hubs are in delivering on these discursive aspirations is unclear. Much in the literature confirms that the establishment of hubs continues despite the lack of evidence proving their efficacy in delivery on discursive aspirations (Friederici, 2018; Pollio, 2020). These aspirations are often related to neoliberal models of economic growth that some argue are contradictory to the values of community and steady learning (Jiménez and Zheng, 2021: 11). Despite 'community' being a core value driving the establishment of hubs, the need for funding and pressure to deliver on broader expectations around entrepreneurial development create an uneasy tension between the technology-led discourse and localized, bottom-up instances of empowerment.

The literature and my discussions with local entrepreneurs in Nairobi[5] raised issues surrounding financial viability, as well as the authenticity of these spaces as being representative of local energies and interests: '"Community" is still used as a concept, but it is often missing the original notion that community members are the ones owning and shaping the hub' (Friederici, 2018: 207). Nevertheless, hubs can be seen as nodal spaces where various spatial circuits intersect, including metropolitan settings, national policy and economic frameworks, and local cultural contexts, informed by the aspirations and lived experiences of participants. They are relational spaces (Jiménez and Zheng, 2021). The sense of permanence and camaraderie is critical to creative collaborative work (Toivonen and Friederici, 2015). Events like hackathons and hosting guest speakers enhance contact between practitioners that would not normally meet. Physical spaces echo the intentions of openness and sharing through communal spaces. Many hubs also offer mentoring and skills-sharing sessions (Jiménez and Zheng, 2021). These opportunities offer an engagement with a global community of people and ideas. Digital hubs aspire to offer members access to a global community of innovators and leaders. Research shows that participants find local networking highly beneficial and welcome the opportunity for access to relatively cheap working spaces.

What some appear to question is how effective hubs are in delivering on local aspirations and whether they represent local cultural and social ways of being in the digital world, as opposed to simply offering a respite from infrastructure failure. I believe a clue may be found in research done by Rosenberg and Brent (2020: 817), where they probed respondents on possible aspirations to relocate to Konzo Tech City, the smart city development on the outskirts of the city: 'Given the close-knit and supportive nature of the technology community in Nairobi, many felt that moving to Konza City would either remove the benefits they were experiencing of being spatially close to the community, or that Konza would destroy the community itself'. My own discussions with respondents revealed that while new developments that offered high-end distribution and communication infrastructure, such as Konza Tech City, were highly attractive to larger corporate firms, fledgling tech entrepreneurs value the interaction and proximity offered by city hubs.[6]

GoDown: hybrid terrains for social engagement, culture and community

I first encountered Joy Mboya, Director of GoDown Arts Centre in Nairobi, when she spoke at an event at my university in Cape Town, where, surrounded by architecture and city-planning students, she extolled the virtues of using an artistic space to connect the city. A couple of years later, I met with her and some of her colleagues in Nairobi in 2020, where we discussed how this endeavour may include the digital realm. Our discussions skirted around the COVID-19 pandemic. A couple of months later, the digital realm would become critical to the functioning of creative professionals in Nairobi and elsewhere. More recently, at a virtual discussion as part of an online event entitled ResiliArt,[7] Mboya facilitated a discussion with several creatives on the interface between the digital ecosystem and the creative economy after COVID-19. The prognosis at this latter discussion was not hopeful: the digital space for making art is not accessible in general, with those who already have a digital presence having a distinct advantage. Smartphone and computer ownership affordability, data costs, and Internet stability were noted as challenges. Nevertheless, the efforts of local telecommunications companies (such as Safaricom, the originator of M-Pesa) in creating data bundles that are affordable does provide some form of levelled access. Adapting to the circumstances of the consumers is commendable, according to panellist, Nanjira Sambuli, a former research manager at the iHub in Nairobi. However, there are more nuanced aspects that need to be addressed, especially in relation to the Internet ecosystem and the commodification of its elements, including its sea-cable infrastructure. The Silicon Valley ethos of radical innovation, typified by the adage 'move fast and break things', is problematic for who it leaves behind and the societal ramifications of innovations 'at all cost'.[8] The digital ecosystem is increasingly being colonized by corporate interests and therefore curtails the effective online functioning of the creative economy.

Perhaps the most appropriate way to make sense of how digital platforms enhance cultural practices as a form of citizenship is to use the GoDown Centre's physical interactions as a starting point. The centre was first established in 2003 in an industrial area on the edges of the city's CBD, maximizing access while optimizing the space afforded by prior industrial land uses. The vision for the centre, however, stretches beyond the crumbling services and dilapidated former car workshops of Dunga Road, just south of Nairobi's railway station. Envisioned as a community anchor for artists and creatives, the vision was to create a pan-African cultural institution that connects artists with other artists and consumers, while also acting as an activator of fledgling talent. A planned, revived GoDown Centre is envisaged as a cultural precinct, where the emphasis is on the city. The aim has been, and is, to create a 'meaningful and symbiotic' relationship with the city,[9] investing in cultural infrastructure.

In the centre's history, the moment that illustrated this relationship with, and to, the city most poignantly was the *Nai Ni Who* ('Who is Nairobi?') campaign in 2013. A community-created multisite arts festival, it was driven by 'allowing people into processes and making space to provide input' (Mboya, quoted in Myers, 2015: 342). In a seminar hosted by the African Centre for Cities, Mboya speaks of the ability of cultural place-based networking in enabling citizenship and a sense of belonging, providing a more rounded understanding of the African urban citizen.[10] Being part of this process of city making, or making sense of the city, through cultural expression enables self-reflection and an exploration of the notion of the public. How, then, does this translate into the virtual realm? Discussions with Mboya and some of her staff revealed an intricate scaffolding of digital expression, activism and campaigning. This includes using digital platforms for showcasing the visual and performance arts, an interactive web site and ongoing engagement with artists that work in the digital space. Jim Chuchu, a filmmaker and artist based in Nairobi, and Matua Matheka, an architect and photographer, are two artists that are part of this expansive artist community with a strong digital presence.

What the *Nai Ni Who* initiative proved was that the role of arts and culture is in creating an identity, valuing yourself and knowing who you are, but the physical infrastructure to enable these expressions is expensive and not necessarily listed in state budgets. The funding campaign for the construction of a new physical infrastructure on the GoDown site uses the hashtag #godowntransforms to tag fly-through videos, downloadable plans, social media posts and so on. The fly-through video of the new centre ends with a provocative invitation to become part of the 'transformation of Kenya's cultural future'.[11] It is to this imagination of what is possible that the discussion now turns.

Afrofuturism's significance as a cultural practice

In a blog post on the GoDown web site, the author speaks to a young scholar on the art that he had donated to the #GoDownTransforms funding drive as the outcome of a school arts week initiative. The theme of the week was Afrofuturism, which the young scholar describes as follows: 'Afrofuturism is about the future, the past and the present. When you combine the future and the past you make Afrofuturism. It's an awesome word! It makes you think of robots in the future with afros! It gives you a kind of burst of creativity.'[12]

My first exposure to this genre was at an exhibition of student work at the South Africa National Arts Festival in Grahamstown in 2018. I found it fascinating how school learners interpreted the future as a mix of old and new, addictive and empowering, with a fascinating combination of traditional African cultural references and fantasy imagery.

Afrofuturism originated from the African diaspora and highlights the artistic work of African, Afro-Latino and African American artists who engage with new technologies and imagine futures while celebrating their cultural identity and heritage. The genre is perhaps most widely known for the science fiction of Octavia Butler, but more recent activist-inspired artistic expressions reveal the power of telling stories of hopeful futures while acknowledging the past: 'critical utopias and storytelling are active participants in reshaping the world by feeding new social models and provocations to the larger population' (Baumann, 2018: 265).

Science fiction, or telling stories about the future, with technology as an actor, engages the collective imagination and is a powerful activist tool. Baumann (2018) refers to Brown's work in Detroit on propagating community gardens, where Brown is interested in how small individual actions lead to collective organizing and can contribute to community building that can then impact at a broader scale. NU's and the CANs' work in Cape Town adopt a similar approach, but what is poignant about these examples is how stories of the future are appropriated. However, in doing so, Afrofuturism also looks to the past by deconstructing and decolonizing the dominant narratives regarding African histories. It is speculative and critical. As a lens for examining blackness and technology, it offers an imagination of the future that places Africans at the centre of technology use and design.

Of course, there is a questioning of Afrofuturism's African-ness given its origins in the diaspora: 'Unlike what it suggests, Afrofuturism has nothing to do with Africa, and everything to do with cyberculture in the West', Bristow (2012: 25) argues. Yet, it does challenge the centrality of Western world views of technology, decentring and decentralizing interpretations of the past and formulations of the future as informed by technology, using cultural practices and techno-culture. Afrofuturism speaks to the diaspora but acknowledges and employs African forms of storytelling and myth making. While the 'African-ness' of Afrofuturism is open to question, the consensus appears to be that its application in technology as a medium and techno-culture through art and music is a move away from the dominance of Western interpretations, decentralizing identity and the generalized accounts of African culture. As Vergès (2017: 46) argues: 'The digital revolution is not only bothering us in terms of a hegemony of an economy that has proved to be unsustainable, but that it continues to impose its worldview.'

Afrofuturism as method, or as sensibility, is a means through which the diversity of the African experience can inform theorizing about the future. The aims are to rewrite history in a way that is mindful of the African voice, to depart from the master–slave framework and to explore future possibilities for positive experiences of blackness (Baumann, 2018). This conceptualization speaks to a transactional and dynamic conceptualization of culture that departs from binaries of inclusion–exclusion when it comes to digital engagement. It acknowledges agency as an 'understanding of culture as practice' when interpreted and influenced by the STS literature (Burrell, 2012: 8).

Afrofuturist urban futures: from utopia to the 'go-slow'

The work of Butler and other authors inspired by Afrofuturism reconstructs the notion of utopia as an idea that can be created from the bottom up, where protagonists negotiate the dystopic and catastrophic present in order to imagine a vision of technology-inspired futures that speak to their own hopes and aspirations (Baumann, 2018). This departs from the ways through which smart city utopias are being imagined by national governments and MNCs. In a type of helicopter urbanism, African fantasies have very little to do with the historical heritage of African urban spaces (Watson, 2013), or, indeed, the dreams, hopes and ambitions of its residents for the future. This speculative, future-oriented component removes the urgency of designing cities for today's problems, focusing on the notion of alternative possible futures based on more social, psychological and emotional aspects that tend to be missing from discussions of urban technology. In fact, the images that accompany these proposals are generally produced in drawing offices in London or Dubai and share an eerie similarity in their visual elements. As argued in Chapter 1, the African smart city visual discourse has very little to do with the actual African city.

In the smart cities visual narrative, there is no informality; rather, highways connect tall skyscrapers and tree-lined boulevards are filled with well-heeled pedestrians making their way to their high-tech jobs. The shack settlements, informal traders and street water sellers all disappear. Roads are wide and unencumbered. This could be Dubai, Hanoi or Lagos. There is no sense of place or history. Public space is manicured and simply a decorative element that provides balanced relief from the proliferation of glass-clad skyscrapers.

Architect and visual artist Olalekani Jeyifous depicts public spaces as spaces of invention and remaking, where remaking and recycling transform infrastructures and high-tension cable masts are appropriated as urban architecture. In his video project, entitled 'Shanty-Megastructures', he combines the aesthetics of informal settlements and shantytowns with the visual language of megastructures. By doing this, Jeyifous brings visibility and dignity to marginalized communities, foregrounding their conditions of inadequate services, which he describes as 'somewhat dystopian' (Jeyifous, quoted in Cheang, 2016). Images of slums are combined with megastructure architecture to convey a future that is intertwined with nature and interspersed with images of the signals of a mobile and online life in the present, such as billboards advertising mobile phone services and online shopping.

Jeyifous explores the subaltern agency that infuses spaces like Makoko, a shantytown on water in Lagos, to their extremes. Residents in Makoko use water as a form of transport, use compacted waste for land reclamation and build bridges and walkways from waste timber. These technologies are depicted in his work as part of megastructures that share space with natural systems and single-storey shacks. Residents continue to move through the city in a milieu that is global and metropolitan in a 'future where technology, urbanism, and capitalism are taken to their technologized, highly segregated extremes' (Cheang, 2016: 419). A poignant quality of the visual imagery is how the past, or tradition, is combined with the urban problems of the present, as represented in the informal lack of suitable infrastructure, with technology underpinning the visions of the future. Cultural, technological and political structures are reinterpreted in a visual language that is dystopian and aspirational. There is also an insidious quality to how the informal 'creeps' into the spaces between buildings, on top of skyscrapers and on building terraces, connected through suspended walkways and waterways in-between. Nature features in interesting ways, such as in forms of reuse and reappropriation.

Jeyifous does not romanticize the informal as a self-organizing and interstitial alternative to corporate urbanism. In two written pieces – one his own and another an interview – he stresses the importance of engaging failure, what he refers to as 'the Abiku phenomenon' (Cheang, 2016), a Yoruba myth that refers to child-like spirits that disrupt the process of reincarnation by inhabiting a young child and compelling them to die at a young age. Thus, the process of cyclical life, birth, life, death, returning to the ancestors and repeat, is disrupted. In many ways, it disrupts the notion of death and replacement, or repeated iterations of the past in a layered unfolding of history. Jeyifous refers to Nigeria's postcolonial past, as well as its present and future, in this regard. What seemingly fails also motivates a break in a perpetual pattern of postcolonial evolutions that are constantly wanting to remake the past. The disorder of the informal is not wished away with glossy utopian imagery, but an agent in determining new definitions of public and private spaces.

A mash-up culture emerges from what might be perceived to be a mess amid order. In his renderings, he uses the 'Quick Paint' architectural rendering software, generating and superimposing new architectural forms on existing buildings and informal interstices. However, he perceives 'Quick Paint' to be 'failed software' given that it does not accurately overlay on vectorized drawings, having little quantifiable functionality other than providing a visual overlay. In the same way that 'Quick Paint' does not redo or reorder the underlying drawing, the Abiku phenomenon refuses to engage the order of things and culturally disrupts traditional narratives. Thus, Jeyifous uses it to construct a spatial language that explores failure and aspiration in the urban.

One of the failures of urban systems in Lagos is its traffic situation, or what locals refer to as the 'go-slow'. In Jeyifous' images, his mash-up includes intertwining networks of elevated walkways, planted with greenery, while waterways underneath suggest transportation by boats and canoes. They are raised above deadlock traffic.

Nnedi Okarofor, a Nigerian author living in the US, uses the 'go-slow' as a backdrop in a short story that also uses Yoruba mythology, entitled 'The go-slow' (Okarofor, 2010). It tells the story of a famous, highly desired male actor, Nkem, on his way to a tryst and his encounter with a strange flock of birds that interrupts his journey while stuck in gridlock traffic. On his journey, we are introduced to the *okadas* (West African motorcycle taxis) that snake their way through the traffic, dodging opportunistic hawkers selling their wares to drivers and passengers in stalled vehicles, and a busy market where colourfully clad women sell Nigerian street food. We are exposed to the smoke-belching trucks and the rust van full of choir members from a fanatical church that the protagonist sees as highly problematic (Okarofor, 2010).

In the description of the 'go-slow', the reader is exposed to the textures, colours and resigned frustrations typically experienced in the notorious Lagos traffic. Nkem's escapist reverie about his pending appointment with his 'destructive distraction' (as he terms his mistress) is interrupted by a small flock of giant birds, emus. One attacks his car, but he hits another, and thinking he has killed it, he puts it in the car boot. Two miles later, with the other birds running alongside his car, he hears a noise in his boot and realizes the emu is not dead. Upon opening his boot, a tall, strong woman wearing a dress that resembles a bird's feathery hide emerges, named Ogaadi (Okarofor, 2010). What follows is a narrative that skilfully weaves the confrontation between bird-woman and protagonist with the ongoing features of urban life: bystanders film it with their mobile phones, hawkers give commentary and the go-slow continues. Nkem reflects on his life with his interloper and realizes that while he did not want to die, he wanted to leave his life behind. Ogaadi offers him an alternative: she turns him into an eagle soaring above the chaos but reminds him to avoid his spirit friends that embodied a number of animals that almost killed him as a child. The spirit friends are companions in the spirit world but could not experience the physical world and therefore sought the companionship of their peers. Ogaadi and Nkem are both *ogbanjes*, seeking freedom from the material world yet forming part of it.

Mythology and the natural world are intertwined with the urban and visceral in this fantasy story. In Jeyifous' work, he is inspired by the Abiku phenomenon in his exploration of failure and aspirations. In both artists' work, grief and tragedy are reversed through the deployment of myth. Communities, kinships and friendships materialize in the voids left by neglect. Jeyifous refers to the self-organizing features of those living in Makoko, for example, who develop sustainable practices out of need: using waste as a means to land reclamation and layering rubbish, sawdust and sand to make islands for schools and homes. He refers to instances of innovation that include the making of bricks out of PVC pipes, plastic containers and nylon pellets. In the stories created by Jeyifous' computer imagery and Okarofor's words, hope and renewal surface as threads throughout the depictions of infrastructure failure, marginal livelihoods and corporate greed. It is to these renewal practices that I turn for the final section of this chapter.

Culture as repair and practice

The lifespan of an object is informed by geography: 'Whilst in the West a cracked screen can mean death; elsewhere, it opens up possibilities for reuse' (Mattern, 2018). The 'culture of repair' is an unassailable part of the landscape in cities of the Global South. Where inherited colonial infrastructures and postcolonial investments meet, much stands in the way of enabling the well-oiled, networked infrastructure: declining public funds; unanticipated population growth; and, no doubt, infrastructure standards that are not necessarily suitable or desirable for contemporary African urban living.

Settled into the maze of such utilities are networks of maintenance and repair that reflect 'the importance of human labour and ingenuity' (Graham and Thrift, 2007: 4) in the continuous restoration of the urban fabric. Repair requires solution and, by extension, invention; as Graham and Thrift (2007) posit, the incremental process of problem-solving that comprises maintenance and repair requires ongoing learning and experimentation. In the same way that the Abiku myth undermines the notion of the new replacing the old, remnants of older tech are remade into the new, not a process of rebirth, just steady but effective tinkering.

Whether through adapting buildings to suit specific needs, repurposing old mobile phones or illegally tapping into electricity lines, the necessity of invention is sometimes an inadvertent effect of infrastructure failure or collapse. Described by Corwin (2018: 14) as 'economies of reuse and repair', the reuse of electronic waste forms an integral part of the informal economy, or, in fact, the 'mainstream' economy, as people use considerable skills to repair and reinvent electronic goods. In Kenya, Cross and Murray (2018) examine how instead of perceiving of broken solar infrastructure as waste, parts and components are reused and repurposed, underpinned by economic networks and local practices, and expanding to the use of new materials and components. Opportunities for agency and innovation abound in the refurbishment of computers and the second-hand trade of technology in Accra, Ghana, due to what Burrell describes as 'some odd and novel surprises in technology's circulation and interpretation' that proliferate in contexts where repair is the only option due to affordability and availability (Burrell, 2012: 6).

City making cannot be reduced to algorithms (Mattern, 2018). The remaking of the city inevitably confronts the need for maintenance and fixing. While notions of innovation and smart redevelopment are tempting in urban conditions where infrastructure is crumbling and outdated, the notion of maintenance – 'the collective project of repair' – appears to be a fitting counter to conventional narratives of innovation (Mattern, 2018). These practices form part of cityscapes currently and feature in the Afrofuturist narratives discussed earlier. Repair is about confronting the past and looking towards the future.

Conclusion

In many ways, the vignettes and stories discussed in this chapter contribute to a broadening of the definition of the public, and of citizenship, to include platforms and physical realms often ignored in mainstream accounts of the city. The informal places that do not appear on a map, the African myths that are omitted from futurist visions and the technology waste that is wished away are not only included in these accounts, but also central to how city futures are imagined. The use of platform tools to map Kibera is combined with other forms of offline media to continuously define and redefine this area as a place that belongs on official maps and in the public consciousness. Innovation hubs are physical places for connection and networking, which is sometimes more important than the discursive goals of the global knowledge economy. Users use it for connection and networking on their own terms. Public life is enhanced and remediated through GoDown's cultural outreach, where the digital realm is a part of this endeavour but not central to it. A core part of the centre's future plans is to be a cultural precinct that informs and engages the city's pulse. This future is already present online, with the pandemic forcing many of its exchanges and fundraising for the future centre into cyberspace.

The activities of MapKibera, the technology hubs and the GoDown Centre all contribute to a public imagination that claims the informal, the unofficial and the marginal as part of the city. Rather than reading the 'public realm' as a space that is defined and sectioned off, either by the technology elite in cyberspace or by the state in physical terms, these examples show that the public realm is dynamic, relational and, in some ways, negotiable. It is a hybrid space, where analogue and digital platforms rub up against each other. It is shown to be collectively created and impacts the physical parameters of public life through movement and place making – through inhabiting and defining features that matter locally.

The value of thinking through the lens of Afrofuturism is the opening of a creative practice that is culturally and visually disruptive. It creates an imaginary and conceptual space for an imagined future that is in conversation with the place-based qualities of African cities, where informality, neglect and infrastructure failure are included in the visions of the future. Dystopian visual languages combine with mythology to illustrate technology-enhanced futures that reflect many African identities, both on the continent and beyond. The decentring and decentralizing functions of this genre enable an artistic appropriation of technology that is infused with hope. As Womack (2013: 42) argues: 'The audacity of hope, the bold declaration to believe, and clarity of vision for a better life and world are the seeds to personal growth, revolutionized societies, and lifechanging technologies.' What the various cultural practices discussed here bring to this dynamic is a bold exchange with the African city on its own terms.

7

Conclusion: On Understanding Situated Platform Urbanism

Disrupted African cities: an introduction and a conclusion

The practices documented in the previous four chapters span an array of interventions that draw on a wide range of technological and social strategies. Many of these are informed by the current platform infrastructure that enables a more distributed agency. I would argue that this differs from what some authors may have had in mind when the notion of technological leapfrogging in Africa was first pronounced. In the mid- to late 1990s, when several authors first starting exploring the impact of telecommunications on cities (Warf, 1995; Graham and Marvin, 1996), many African countries were recovering from structural adjustment policies. The forced reduction of public spending on social infrastructure, the retreat of the state and the emphasis on economic growth had an adverse impact on livelihoods and social services (Fonjong, 2014; Konadu-Agyemang, 2000). South Africa was in its democratic nascency, and while it had significant advantages in relation to telecommunications infrastructure, a slow and confused deregulation transition frustrated efforts at enabling ubiquitous Internet access (Lewis, 2005). It is not entirely inaccurate to argue that most African countries joined the information revolution on the back foot and that the leapfrogging phenomenon was an overestimation.

The emphasis on technology as a development tool is inevitable and, in many ways, a continuation of a discourse that embraces ICT as a means to modernization (Schech, 2002; Moodley, 2005). Fortunately, the ICT4D area of work has broadened and become more granular in its analysis of tech appropriation among Africans, but technological determinism still permeates bilateral and national policy discourses. While the notion of technological determinism has become somewhat *passé* in STS, it is still very much visible in public discourse and developmental aid – the idea that 'development is propelled by K & T [knowledge and technology]' (Cherlet, 2014: 775).

In his discussion of the evolution of development discourses in relation to knowledge and technology transfer, Cherlet explores the genealogy of two determinisms in this regard: technological and epistemic. This dynamic is more recently discernible in smart city proposals, where engineering and technology multinationals offer pre-packaged solutions to urban problems. Work by African scholars and others has placed emphasis on the contextual nuances of digital adoption, however (Pollio, 2019, 2020; Guma, 2020; Odendaal, 2020). This book builds on this work and consolidates much of what has been written on the topic, with the further aim of expanding and diversifying the literature on platform urbanism.

Much has changed over the last 20 years as the themes in academic debates have transitioned from smart cities, to smart urbanism and now platform urbanism. I recall attending an International Society of City and Regional Planners (ISoCaRP) conference in 2001, cheekily entitled 'Honey I Shrunk the Space', excited at the prospect of Bill Mitchell's keynote. It was days after the attack on the World Trade Centre in New York City in September 2001, and his presentation was done on Skype due to his inability to travel from the US. The scratchy reception and interrupted sound quality in the plenary space reflected the panic and uncertainty, in fact, the disconnection, the audience felt after such a heinous and disruptive event. Some 20 years later, we find ourselves in a pandemic that has isolated communities, caused immense suffering and robbed millions of people of their dreams and futures. Technology has definitely enabled economies to function and many jobs to be secured. The smartphone has become ubiquitous and online connection is a part of our social and professional lives, especially since March 2020. The exponential growth in technology innovation and platform expansions simply cannot be underestimated. As Anthony Townsend (2013: 3) quipped in his *Smart Cities* book: 'We'll never know what tipped the balance – perhaps a new city bus fired up its GPS tracker for the first time, or some grad students at Massachusetts Institute of Technology (MIT) plugged their coffee pot into Facebook. But at some point the Internet of people gave way to the Internet of Things.'

Not many of the vignettes I have examined and discussed in this book could be termed groundbreakingly innovative in the conventional sense. Many have received international accolades in the past (for example, MapKibera and M-Pesa), as well as attention in the academic and the popular press. In this book, I display them both as examples of local smart solutions to urban problems and as components of a patchwork of initiatives that respond to the urgencies of place. Some of them are based on ideas from elsewhere, informed by scientific advances and technology solutions from other parts of the world that are repurposed for local conditions. What makes these vignettes endogenous is that the problem to be solved was locally defined and analysed, and the platforms were refined or developed locally, applied to situated issues, and evolved to adjust to changes. Some of these initiatives received input and funding from outside Africa; in some cases, the catalytic inputs were from outside. However, what makes them local is that they were driven, contextualized and embedded by Africans, and very much informed by the qualities of the spaces they are located in; in other words, they are situated.

However, the main question that informs this book is: how does platform urbanism contribute to systemic changes in African cities? It is an important question because not only does it address some of the substantive issues that will impact on the future of African urban spaces, but it is also intended to disrupt the notion of smart cities by offering a different picture or definition of the term. In this array of disruptive examples and small innovations, I believe, are hints at how cities in Africa can determine a more sustainable and just future by harnessing digital platforms. The four themes – mobility, food security, social mobilization and public culture – were intended to capture some of the main challenges of cities on the continent. In essence, they cover the spatial, economic, cultural and political dimensions of urban spaces, as well as pick up on some of the contemporary urban studies debates. The lens that was used to make sense of these vignettes is informed by STS and African urbanism, and this work also shows how to take the postcolonial STS area of work further. Freetown, Kampala, Nairobi, Zanzibar and Cape Town are not entirely representative of the continent, but the vignettes explored share a number of contextual realities that are representative of African cities. The focus on contingency, emergence, associational life, informality and remaking speak to the formation of alternative modernities or urban configurations that impact the blending of global technologies with local practices. STS is essentially focused on how technologies and their locations co-produce and co-constitute each other (Harding, 2016). Postcolonial STS emphasizes modes of analysis and new critiques that consciously emerge from the consideration of the relationship between technology and society as a process of co-production of culture, economic processes and group identities (Anderson, 2002). This undermines the notion of smart as new and revolutionary; rather, it is another ingredient in the ongoing adventure of contemporary urbanism. In making sense of what this looks like in relation to technology disruption, in the following four parts, I examine how platform urbanism is situated in the African urban context. The first part examines the dynamics of space and the value of place as a source of information on the functioning, features and character of digital platforms. The second related focus is on flow and connection as functions of these spatial relationships. The global–local dynamic is a familiar theme in popular and academic work on technology and cities, but I am more interested in the connections that are driven and anchored by local actors on their own terms, and how this then impacts on African urban spaces. The third, and in some ways also related, focus concerns the governance contexts and regulatory systems that frame the extent to which digital platforms operate. This is also an opportune moment to reflect on emerging regimes that may shift the governance environment in future. In the fourth part, I am interested in the relations of trust and continuity that are nurtured in platform-driven interventions, and how that may impact on urban futures.

The recurrent focus on spatial relationships evolves from a reflection on the vignettes, but it is also intentional. Philip, Irani and Dourish (2012) argue that the cultural dynamics of place are under-studied in STS, and I would agree with that. I also concur with Furlong (2010) when she contends that STS tend to privilege the technical at the expense of the more nuanced dynamics of socio-political processes. I would argue that the examples in this book show that in the urban milieu, political struggles are ever present in the qualities of places and the spatial relationships that define them. The 'local' can be rendered quite abstract, devoid of geographic and temporal specificity, when simply expanding the repertoire of STS case studies to the Global South without understanding and engaging the dynamics of place. Doing so requires different questions to be asked, in which technology appropriation is approached as a complex practice of translation and appropriation, moving away from blanket solutions and generalized readings of technical systems. Philip, Irani and Dourish (2012: 9) refer to 'hybrid knowledge practice' as a frame for understanding power, history, identity and epistemology as part of the STS story. In this book and more recent work on African smart urbanism, practices and strategies are understood in relation to context, and alternative forms of knowledge generation and agency are examined. Evolving from the themes in relation to the vignettes is cyborg activism and engagement that allows for connection and problem solving in unexpected ways. I prefer to engage with it as a hybrid form of urban life, where the old and new, the social and technical, and the past, present and future are combined. The conclusion to this work is to focus on the ideas of hybridity and constellation as concepts to be taken forward in future research. These socio-technical constellations are hopeful extensions of the public imagination and methods of collective sense making.

The many textures of African platform urbanism

The idea of disruption has become part of a lexicon of terms used to encapsulate manifestations of the knowledge-based economy and, in some ways, late capitalism. In the African context, the associated glamour is expressed in fantasy proposals and expanded hopes and predictions based on flimsy evidence. Whether it is the iHub in Nairobi or ride-hailing apps there and in other parts of East Africa, how these corporate rationalities that drive the proliferation of digital platforms land in cities is uneven, messy and sometimes surprising. If disruption is to be defined as 'the act of stopping something from continuing in the normal way',[1] then I believe it to be imperative to revisit what 'the normal' way is in African cities, or what the shared features are on such a large and diverse continent.

Many of the expected issues came up: the ubiquitous functioning of the informal economy; uneven governance frameworks; infrastructure failure; and the profound impact of the COVID-19 pandemic on livelihoods – yet another shock for households that, in many cases, have been exposed to violence, famine, past epidemics like Ebola and state oppression. In the face of such overwhelming factors, it is nonsensical to expect platforms to make a substantive difference. Yet, I would argue, in the preceding chapters are indications of practices that can shift and edge cities towards being more inclusive and sustainable, perhaps in unexpected ways. However, the agency that drives meaningful change is distributed and in constant negotiation with the factors that inform regimes, or the larger governance and social landscapes that frame city functioning. This propensity to act, or to impact, is informed by place and the dynamics of space.

Space and place

In Chapter 2, I spent some time exploring space, place and agency in platforms when highlighting the need for understanding platform landings in situ, unpacking landed calibrations, the interface with local survival networks and local regulations specifically related to land use and spatial relationships. There is a co-generative dynamic between platforms and urban life, but in some cases, I would argue that the old spatial constraints related to movement and proximity are still relevant. There are nevertheless some insights that give clues as to how platforms can recombine urban places towards more representative and inclusive futures.

What strikes me as significant in unpacking the relationship between the place-based dynamics of urban spaces and how they are regulated is the absolute lack of sensitivity or cognizance of the 'everyday' experiences of place-making by policymakers. In the vignettes discussed, this relates to the informal economy. Almost all the examples discussed in this book address informality through economic linkages (Twiga and Yebo Fresh), mapping and data gathering (MapKibera and the SLURC), and as an important informant to civic action (NU, CANs and the SLURC). Recognition that the informal economy and the lack of housing that leads to the proliferation of shack settlements are integral parts of the African city is not a new theme in the literature on African urbanism. However, what these cases illustrate is that the incorporation of digital platforms into economic processes, such as the distribution of food, as well as into mobility systems and forms of civic activism, allows, in fact, demands, that the informal be included. Different interpretations of the same platform can land in different sets of spatial relations in different contexts, but I would argue that a ubiquitous feature of African urbanism and, by extension, African platform urbanism is the recognition and inclusion of the informal.

Of course, where a platform chooses to land is also associated with the lack of local regulation in relation to informality, as well as gig workers. This does impact on how platform urbanism manifests. However, it also creates opportunities for exploring new regulatory and thereby physical spaces. Experimentation with drone technology in Zanzibar. for example, was given more space due to a fledgling set of regulations being negotiated. The double-edged sword is that while lack of regulation can inspire invention, it can also lead to externalities that have place-based impacts.

The failure of the state to intervene meaningfully or effectively in the functioning of places is what contributed to the evolution of many of the platforms discussed. In the SafeBoda example, it was safety and the need for professionalism that led to the creation of the app in the first place. Much of the official antagonism towards the sector is associated with road safety and what is perceived to be a chaotic and fast-growing traffic of motorcycles on congested roads. As a response, paratransit platforms have embraced a corporate rationality that infuses media and public profiles. SafeBoda claims that it contributes to greater road safety and more responsible conduct of passengers. In some cases, this 'professionalism' or veneer of corporate efficiency does translate into some form of predictability and visibility for drivers and passengers. In the Twiga Foods case, the rationalization of the supply chain through its platform does enhance some form of security for food growers and sellers. The suspicion with which the informal is treated by authorities is often associated with how they manifest in space; the lack of control and order seems to permeate discourses. Platforms like SafeBoda and Twiga do not necessarily change that, but there is a path dependency and some predictability built into these apps that enable some stability for *boda-boda* riders and food sellers that could have longer-term spatial impacts. They can potentially influence new policy, but they also disrupt less official kinship systems that, in some cases, have evolved over a long time. In the case of *boda-boda* bodies, preliminary findings in Kampala show that they disrupt the stage system, which essentially follows a 'hub and spoke' spatial logic, associated with localized governance systems within the *boda-boda* industry. SafeBoda, like some other ride-hailing apps, bring a different form of spatial governance: a centralized digital space in the form of a platform that enables distributed ride pickups that can bypass the stage system completely. Together with others (Esfandari, 2015; Doherty, 2020), my own reading of this dynamic indicates that this is not necessarily a mutually exclusive dynamic, but comes with tensions. This can, of course, change, but it appears that the two coexist, perhaps with some conflict. Spatially, it indicates some transition in future, where one of two sets of relations could evolve. The first is where riders align themselves with a range of platforms to maximize income and use the stages as a base for social networking, local alliances and for picking up non-app rides, thus using a host of strategies to enable a consistent income. This appears consistent with how livelihood strategies are pursued: minimizing risk through diversifying forms of income. The other scenario could be that as apps proliferate, stages (and their governing bodies) associate with particular platforms, leading to a corporatized distribution of *boda-boda* hubs. In some ways, this last scenario does echo the ways through which mobile telephony has overtaken the use of landlines, often referred to in the African context as a form of 'leapfrogging'. From a city perspective, this has led to an 'on-the-go' spatiality that allows for ephemeral connections to place and associational networks across space. The public realm is infused with the presence of mobile companies as enablers of work, life and play.

Thus, there is a literal translation of platform power in the urban realm that results in physical changes to spaces with broader impacts. The activities that permeate urban spaces may now be enabled through digital connection, but the pedestrian still needs to share the pavement with the street vendor, the growth of motorcycle numbers due to the availability of income generation through ride-hail and delivery platforms still demands road maintenance and traffic control, and the intensification of civil society action around homelessness still intensifies awareness and demands for change. Platform urbanism does not replace or lessen the need for infrastructure maintenance and for the state to deliver on its mandate. Rather, I would argue that it increases the need for it, and as in many examples discussed here, it provides an arena for social mobilization around urban needs.

The inadequacy of physical infrastructure and the impacts it has on, for example, food markets, that is, the qualities of place and the neglect of its features, can provide an impetus for digital invention, as in the case of the distribution of food during the pandemic in Cape Town and overcoming inefficiencies of distribution in Cape Town and Nairobi through app-based solutions. In considering the interface between urban infrastructure and digital platforms, the distribution of food becomes a very applicable example. Food also provides a reliable lens for understanding how the roles of the state, civil society and business manifest in relation to space through investment dynamics, land-use planning, transport infrastructure delivery and maintenance, and neighbourhood design. Similarly, the spatial parameters that determine household access are critical: access to transport; the availability of small, manageable portions in a cash economy; and reliable access to nutrition. The platform arena offers some flexibility in responding to niche market demands and allowing for a more granular distribution system. Current applications in many cities are dominated by big supermarket chains; the flexibility afforded by home-delivery apps may skew in favour of middle to upper incomes. Apps that serve informal food sellers and *spaza shop* owners in South Africa, as well as *mama mbongas* and *dukas* in Kenya, use platform capacity for data processing towards a broader market and range of suppliers. They potentially also impact favourably on food security by recognizing diversity in the food value chain.

Yet, what the focus on food shows is that mapping and spatial analysis, that is, the more traditional ways of making sense of the causes of food scarcity, are important. The use of drone technology and associated platforms to map and expose climate change impacts is significant. There is a need for knowledge-based institutions and for government to harness platform technologies towards a public good. The use of drones is contested, however. Again, this is impacted by place-based dynamics, such as local readings of drone threats, the dynamics of gender and traditions, and the regulatory environment for the sharing and extended use of spatial data.

In addition to the marginalization of the informal, the CAN case also shows how the lack of sensitivity to the settlement typologies and spatial dynamics of cities during the initial stages of South Africa's pandemic lockdown had severe repercussions. Having access to data is one thing, but ignoring the implications of such information in the 'control and response' approach taken by the state was utterly irresponsible. Like the example of Twiga, the use of platforms to overcome the spatial tyrannies of infrastructure unevenness and curtailed distribution networks – in this case, due to lockdown measures, as opposed to gradual infrastructure collapse – was significant. WhatsApp, Facebook and Zoom were used to facilitate communication, exchange resources and share information. Overcoming spatial constraints through digital exchange was critical to enabling support within and between communities.

Urban practices and flows, within the limits of land-use planning, regulation and infrastructure design, determine the features and quality of spaces. Much of the work that is done in Freetown and Cape Town, and explicitly so in Kibera, speaks to the definition and designation of place-based features towards a spatial imagination, that is, an identification with place, and, by extension, towards a public imagination of possible urban futures. The remaking of public life through the curated combinations of the digital and physical, and the sharing of experiences across scales in real time enabled through digital platforms, contribute to hybrid, relational spaces. What the value of these are in relation to public life and to future city functioning is not so much that they are more inclusive; while the vignettes in this book show that they can be, many would argue that elements of the digital divide still exist and that there are ongoing barriers to access that may deepen inequalities. Rather, how these spaces differ is that they enable new relations, not easily forged in the past. They enable alliances across socio-economic divides and forge and reinforce shared values. They become nodal points of knowledge generation and identification of place-based issues. They become pedagogical spaces, where exchange of tacit knowledge enables connection. Notwithstanding the critique of innovation hubs as lacking funding and local entrepreneurship, for example, they offer spaces for connection and exchange in an environment that offers improved infrastructure than the norm. CANs enable alliances across socio-economic and spatial barriers; MapKibera provides spatial literacy that reinforces identification with place; and the SPLURC partners with SDI affiliates, local communities and, in some cases, the state to address lack of service access in informal settlements.

These relational spaces are hybrids. They are enabled through a range of digital media, as well as more traditional forms of interaction. They are simultaneously physical, virtual and imagined. In Afrofuturist visual art, the past, present and future are engaged in space: modernism, as accentuated in skyscrapers, is combined with slum technologies to depict a local negotiated spatial future that acknowledges informal place making and reclaims practices as a pathway to re-imagining the future. Much of the literary and visual imagery pays homage to African mythology. Some of it acknowledges practices that remake the old towards a reinvention of the new, such as featured in reclamation and recycling efforts. This does not always make for orderly, manicured places, the desire for which is emblematic of a physical ideal that is informed by 20th-century modernism. This is where the smart city visual rhetoric fails: it is not looking to the future; it is looking back to a past that never existed in African cities. Notwithstanding the smart infrastructure that underpins these futuristic smart city proposals, and the fact that many of them have been, and will be, built, perhaps at a smaller scale and largely on the outskirts of existing cities, Afrofuturism is an imaginative jolt intended to unsettle conventional notions of African relationship to technology and future forms of place making.

Flow and connection

Perhaps surprisingly, arising from the vignettes is a reminder that despite the seemingly ubiquitous nature of digital platforms, the structural limitations of access remain. Within the world of digital flows and expanded platform architectures, there are still physical and socio-economic spaces of disconnection. In addition to being potential platform incubators, technology hubs, for example, also offer a reprieve from interrupted electricity supply and patchy online access. Space matters, and physical constraints do not just disappear at the press of a keyboard. Market inefficiencies arise as a result of adequate distribution infrastructure or the failure and lack of maintenance of physical connectivity, as illustrated in the example of the costs of a banana in the Twiga example. In the distribution of food, physical transportation is critical, though also reliant on information on market trends and availability.

The operability of a platform and data capacity do, indeed, enable more efficient distribution processes.

Marginal places can also be the start of broader spatial connections, such as the GoDown Centre's efforts to enrol and include the citizens of the city of Nairobi in its future cultural explorations. Using a combination of online and offline presences, the 'Who is Nairobi?' campaign was very successful in enabling a sense of belonging through cultural place-based networking, augmented through online video and social media. Of course, a more critical view would also reveal the dark side of platform urbanism of reduced autonomy and disconnection, as expressed in the discussion on the GoDown Centre. The online space for food distribution and sales, for example, can have an eerie resemblance to the physical distribution of incomes. The pandemic revealed the very cruel ramifications of social exclusion in Sierra Leone and Cape Town, for example. Restricting informal trade and *spaza shops* in Cape Town (and other South African cities), as well as limiting economic activity and job access, led to hunger in the city's most remote neighbourhoods. It also led to loss of connection within neighbourhoods.

The CAN initiative is significant, in that it used platforms to connect and inform, but also recognized the dark side of social media by using a set of values – or 'ways of working', as CTT refers to them – that provide the parameters for connection and engagement. This 'bounded' web of relations is intended to accommodate the diversity that is inherent in the city and within many of its neighbourhoods. The platforms were also utilized towards connecting across neighbourhoods and thereby facilitating shared projects. While I am reluctant to overemphasize the cross-cultural and cross-income associational networks that were enabled through digital means, I nevertheless found that some of those connections had not existed before, for better or for worse, and that some form of shared understanding and experience of the fallout of a pandemic is a step towards a shared urban experience. None of these exchanges happen cold or are solely enabled through technology. Existing associational networks do feature and inform how the digital expands and deepens. However, the CAN example, in particular, shows potential for new networks and alliances. Collective sense making of a crisis like COVID-19 does take established social groups outside their comfort zones.

The expansive potential of apps, largely enabled through platform architectures and centralized data storage, does reveal opportunities for addressing livelihoods through an extension of tech functionality. The expanded offerings of SafeBoda to include the sale of local foods, food delivery during the pandemic, the offer of insurance options to drivers and the sale of airtime online are, I believe, significant. So too is the expansion of Twiga functionality to include loss of income insurance, for example. The fact that M-Pesa exists as a financial tool that often underpins the use of apps in Kenya is an indication of its functionality as much as it is of its cultural acceptance and sustained use. Focusing on the mobile phone as a form of infrastructure, that is, as an artefact that connects and remits, is a critical feature of smart and platform African urbanism. In fact, without it, there would be no such things as the smart African city. Affordable access to data emerged as one of the most critical factors in almost all the examples discussed. There is a small irony in the fact that not only is the enrolment of informal actors and those advocating for the homeless into the mainstream enabled through the corporate sector, but the constraints on those operating on the very edges of the socio-economic spectrum are also in the hands of multinational mobile phone companies. The state simply does not appear to feature in this dynamic, other than through regulation.

The corporate environment of platforms does lend itself to partnerships and economic expansion. Many of the examples started with angel funding and then attracted private capital as the business model proved itself. Expansion also means partnerships across country boundaries, such as Relog and Twiga. Embedded interoperability through social platform expansions impacted NU's use of these tools. The socio-technical dynamic is very relevant where the technical and the social can reinforce each other in both directions. At some point, however, as it impacts city spaces, the relation to the state does become pertinent.

Governance and new regimes

The uneasy relationship between regulators and those making a living in the informal is not going to disappear with the onset of platforms. While the corporate power of platforms enables some form of leverage, especially when aligned with groups that have political currency, such as the *boda-boda* sector in Kampala, the relationship reverts to negotiation, rather than coercion. One of the most telling respondent quotations that I would like to repeat is the one from Ricky Thompson from SafeBoda, who said: "For us as the innovators, we are always ahead of the regulation"; a similar sentiment was echoed in my discussions with drone operators. A policy vacuum does allow for experimentation. However, there is a strong networking element: a process of bricolage and negotiation that often relies on existing power blocks and appeal to broader policies that resonate locally. While it is tempting to see state power as either lacking or used inappropriately, in many of these cases, the expansion of platform urbanism is, at some point, subject to negotiation and lobbying.

The poignant question is: how could these negotiations contribute to regimes that are more inclusive of the informal economy and does the platform contribute to this in any way? It is too early to tell, but indications are that, at the very least, the profile afforded to the *boda-boda* sector through its social media campaign and the safety statistics that indicate an improvement on the norm, coupled with the fact that it forms part of a political lobby group, could pave the way for a more co-productive solution to mobility that recognizes the role played by paratransit. In short, the presence of the platform could lend legitimacy to the sector. The two drone examples used shared a difficulty regarding regulation. In the Zanzibar case, the involvement of the state in partnership with the university provided a secure institutional base for the project. Issues arose around the sharing of data. On mainland Tanzania, there is recognition that the policy vacuum represents an opportunity for influencing regulations in such a way as to establish a regime that fits the technology. In South Africa, a country that was one of the first in the world to formulate a comprehensive regulatory framework for drone use and ownership, the feeling is that it restricts innovation and potential livelihoods. Entering the drone space is expensive and convoluted. The relationship between regulation and innovation is a difficult one. In many ways, it relates to the regulation of informal spaces too. The dilemma is in ensuring appropriate protection of the public interest while allowing for livelihoods and invention. Platform technologies do allow for an expansion of functionality, as well as forms of interoperability that could be harnessed in this regard. This would depend on how the platform business model accommodates things.

Perhaps one of the most practical ways through which regime changes can happen is knowledge co-production and sharing. The collection and processing of data, and their representation in a form that engages policy, is already proving to be effective in Freetown. Also, sometimes the state simply gets it wrong and civil society steps in. Misguided interventions have livelihood impacts, such as lockdown regulations that restrict informal trade, public transport plans that dismiss the role of the paratransit sector or housing interventions that further entrench spatial segregation. These are generally situated in policy regimes that are out of touch with the dynamics of place in African cities, and they are most definitely not in touch with technology-informed urban change. The CAN and NU examples do not provide a comprehensive answer to the failures of the state, but they do give an indication of how civil society organizes and lobbies. In both cases, the use of platforms is flexible yet intentional. In both cases, the relationship with the local state is very uncomfortable and, at times, confrontational, whereas in the SLURC case, data are used to influence policy in a more cooperative way. All these examples speak to a politically astute use of data and social media that holds the state accountable. The gathering and packaging of information is a political act. Sometimes, this can also be as reductive, with the use of infographics, the simplification of messages through the selective use of quantifiable data and the headline messages backed up through numbers. In as much as the state can be strategic in its use of indicators, platforms offer the same functionality to civil society organizations. In the case of MapKibera, it puts informal settlements on the map. In Cape Town, it enables community building and lobbies support from unlikely allies. Drone technology enables an elevated view that exposes inequality. In Freetown, it puts informal communities on the policy agenda. This is not so much a politics of dissensus, to use Kaika's turn of phrase, but a data politics that has an experiential quality that appeals to the broader public. This cyborg activism creates nodes of exchange that are sometimes surprising yet potentially powerful in forging alliances that could inspire meaningful change.

The 'slow burn' that Robins refers to in his work on the Social Justice Coalition in Cape Town and the movement at the 'speed of trust' advocated by CTT run contrary to the outcomes-based numbers game that is generally promoted by the state in relation to development. Yet, these organizations are effective in staying present and relevant through social media and the continuous exchange enabled primarily through WhatsApp. In South Africa, the tension between a civil society movement that constantly chips away at the delivery discourse and a strong state that has mobilized its resources significantly towards output is ongoing and a constant theme in politics. In Sierra Leone, a post-conflict and traumatized state, the opportunity to swing the discourse towards a more sympathetic view of informality, within a larger process of state rebuilding, is being edged forward by collaborative research and knowledge co-production. In Kibera, the consistent mapping of places that matter, constrain and define public life, and provide refuge not only contributes to spatial awareness, but also, I would argue, asserts a form of citizenship that puts slum dwellers on official maps.

Trust and continuity

The landing of apps, or, indeed, their operationalization within the broader urban milieu, is deeply relational and, as discussed, informed by spatial and governance contexts. New forms of 'doing things', whether urban activism, mobility, food distribution or community engagement, coexist with older practices. Regulation can, to some extent, make an impact, but the desire and imperative of pursuing livelihoods will always find pathways to cobble together practices that best suit circumstances.

Platform-enabled practices do not simply replace more established norms; rather, they rely on associational networks, local knowledge and embedded technological cultures. This is what determines opportunities for a digitally assisted urban evolution that responds to local challenges. One of the street traders in the Twiga case attested to the trust that can be gained through predictable and trustworthy service and pricing control. Where storage facilities are scarce, for example, being able to access and exchange data via an app is very useful. Where livelihoods are pursued 'on the move' and contingent upon a diverse range of factors, consistency and transparency are exceptionally important.

The CANs in Cape Town were informed by a spirit of 'moving at the speed of trust', despite the very urgent needs arising from COVID-19. Here, the issue of trust and community formed part of the *raison d'être* of the organization. Ways of working were initially determined by a collective and then used to frame digital interactions. Establishing the issues, needs and opportunities within a community or neighbourhoods was the starting point, which was, of course, enabled through WhatsApp. However, how the other functions of social media were then utilized to expand the network was framed by the interaction.

Exploitative relations in the informal realm are not uncommon in the Global South or North and do veer into the critical sphere. The lack of regulation can lead to corruptive practices that are more aligned with kinship networks than with transparent rules of engagement. Whether considering the syndicates that govern the distribution of produce from small-scale farmers in Kenya or the stage arrangements in Uganda, the lack of state engagement with urban needs, such as mobility and food distribution, has historically opened spaces for abuse and exploitation. Digital platforms add another layer of unauthorized practices that impact the public realm. Whether such platforms enable more formalized and transparent economic relations due to their corporate nature is up for discussion. Certainly, SafeBoda and Twiga embrace forms of individual agency in their promotion of transparency and predictability through their apps. I would agree with Pollio (2019), though, that the rationalities of multinational technology firms seldom overlap with the labour and economic dynamics of African urban spaces. The examples I discuss here are more successful in doing so because they are locally driven and initiated.

Whether apps enable, for example, greater social acceptance of *boda-boda* riders in Kampala or the embrace of social activism as a response to the socio-economic fallout of lockdown during the early days of the COVID-19 pandemic in Cape Town is not entirely clear. Part of the SafeBoda aim is to professionalize the sector in order to create an environment for drivers and passengers that is more predictable and manageable. In the case of CANs, the distance and convenience afforded through apps, as well as the potential anonymity, does lend a voice to more retired personalities, as much as it does online trolls. Yet, there is no hierarchy and no strategic plan or objectives; they are formulated to be decentralized, locally driven and co-productive. They disband when necessary and emerge when needed. Smart features are appropriated in accordance with local needs, and neighbourhood priorities determine which media and platforms are utilized and for what. Moderator volunteers are essential in ensuring that the 'ways of working' are adhered to on social media.

A theme that emerged from the Cape Town cases, in particular, the CANs and NU, was the significance of the legacy of anti-apartheid activism, especially the street committee systems, as well as the lessons learnt during the Treatment Action Campaign in the early post-apartheid years and the more recent 'Fees must Fall' movement at South African universities. Their tacit knowledge and neighbourhood mobilization skills were combined with the distributive power of platforms to mobilize. CANs were effective in combining the efforts of established community organizers with those of inhabitants that had no prior interest in, or experience of, activism. The platforms were adept at creating a neutral space for sharing and exchange, despite some unevenness in relation to data and smartphone access. By all accounts, this did not undermine the efforts of CANs because data access was established as a need and then addressed accordingly.

The cross-neighbourhood networks that some of the CANs participated in facilitated collaboration between poor and rich neighbourhoods. The idea was to collaborate on resource access, stop the spread of misinformation, purchase data and engage in joint projects, one being community gardens in the Seaboard and Gugulethu CANs. Building trust among communities that are generally very suspicious of each other was critical. The technology allowed for continuity and resource exchange that flowed in both directions. Platforms were levellers, as in the absence of usual physical interaction, it could be relied on as a neutral space for the relay of local knowledge and problem solving.

The deployment of storytelling as a form of activism and as a vehicle to represent data is significant in all the cases. It features in the profile of food traders in Kampala, as part of SafeBoda's offerings, in the stories of drivers that led to the formation of BebaBeba, in CAN neighbourhood tales and by the homeless featured in NU's activism, among others. Digital platforms enable a packaging specific to content and the message to be conveyed. These techniques, used to great effect by NU and CANs, are intended to build trust with the larger public, where stories are used to enable some form of identification with people from different walks of life by appealing to a common sense of public good. In Twitter feeds, there are instances of continuity as specific personalities recur. I would argue that the drone photography used by Miller in 'Unequal Scenes' also captures a pictorial story that cannot be argued with; it exists, it is as it is and it cannot be rationalized away. In some ways, it appeals to the senses and evokes an emotional response. I have seen these visuals many times over used by students, policymakers, city planners and politicians to tell the story of segregation. It is, of course, selective and represents a visual discourse, which is part of its power. On the one hand, everyday experiences of the urban poor in Freetown, Nairobi, Cape Town and Kampala are captured in a granular and textured way. On the other, drone photography provides an elevated perspective that tells a more structural story.

Then there is trust in the future, that is, in a collective imagination that captures hopes for urban futures. My (albeit limited) foray into Afrofuturism is intended to get a sense of how technology features in artistic impulses. Cultural practices give some indication of the public imagination. As is noted in the GoDown example, cultural practices contribute to self-reflection and the forging of individual and collective identities. Of interest is the disruptive intention of artistic devices employed by artists to consciously interrupt the continuation of postcolonial cycles of remaking by foregrounding so-called 'failure', using mythology as a written and visual narrative device to challenge the tendency to constantly want to eliminate the past through remaking futures. Disengaging from this means rejecting preconceived notions of technology-infused futures and, like Nkem in Okarofor's short story, connect with the authenticity of self.

Reflections on hybrid smart urbanism

The flows and connections that enable livelihoods, the spaces that results from these dynamics, and the histories, current energies and future hopes that infuse local places all contribute to an urbanity that is constantly in the making. Platform urbanism enables a multidirectional agency that can be enormously powerful yet also very fleeting at times. These reflections unveiled forms of place making and spatial engagement that depart from traditional forms of such and differ vastly from preconceived notions of the smart city. What emerge are a relational sense making of spaces, knowledge generation and procurement that not only contribute to local solutions, but also read the problem collectively – a form of re-description (Simone and Pieterse, 2018). The digital platform is a tool that enables connection and flow, but it is also appropriated to suit the needs of the place. Practices evolve in the everyday as part of the everyday and integrate technology accordingly, which, in itself, opens new possibilities for expansion and exchange. I believe it imperative to examine the notion of hybridity a little more carefully, therefore, as it is more accurate in capturing socio-technical change in cities than simply embracing platform urbanism.

The first dimension of examining hybridity in the constellations that are shaped and informed by disruptive practices is the combination of face-to-face communication and networks, or physical interactions with smart solutions. The line between digital and physical, or between analogue and smart, is constantly negotiated and traversed. The assemblage idea is useful here, as it refers to material, social and, in this case, virtual relations that are assembled and contribute to a collective energy. I am more inclined, like Guma (2020), to use the word 'constellations' to refer to these collective sets of connections. The term 'constellation', if using its astronomy analogy, does refer to a collective energy that grows and attracts with its connective energies. What is visible in the vignettes discussed is that platform architecture allows for additions and expansions that are related to its original purpose and, of course, its business model, with a formulated picture of the end user, and allows for the addition of functions and service providers/actors. In the civil society activism example of CANs and NU, as well as the SLURC to some extent, the boundaries of the constellations that they entail are established by a predetermined set of values and a common purpose shared with others. Here, the platform is not the starting point, as it is arguably with Twiga and SafeBoda (and BebaBeba), but a means, a tool and a platform for physical and electronic exchange. The result in CTT is a Milky Way of sorts: a series of constellations that nevertheless conform to an overall gravitas and spatial delineation. What I find most hopeful about the examples discussed is how the socio-economic edges of cities are enrolled into, what are, in some cases, very diverse, sociocultural and cross-spatial dynamics.

A second dimension of this hybridity, therefore, is the combination of socio-economic and technical dynamics. Many of the digital platforms examined in this book are associated with urban infrastructure: mobility, logistics and shelter are features. Thinking about their impacts takes us beyond the digital realm, therefore, as has been argued in other work on platforms. The play between digital and physical is influenced by temporal, institutional, regulatory and sociocultural dynamics. How SafeBoda lands in Nigeria is different from its base in Uganda, impacted by monetary customs, the regulatory attitude to *okadas*, road systems and the presence and influence of existing ride-hailing companies. The platform paratransit environment that emerges is one that includes all these features.

The expanded idea of 'people as infrastructure' (Simone, 2004) becomes more granular with the conceptual incorporation of platforms as part of the urban realm. The unstable circumstances in which informal traders, drivers and gig workers operate make them vulnerable to corporate exploitation. In some cases, ride-hail drivers have further entrenched their disadvantage by plunging themselves into debt when their platform earnings could not keep up with their car payments. Complaints about long driving hours and reduced profits for drivers are common. Digitalization of functions does make them part of a platform infrastructure that, while more businesslike and backed by investment capital, are part of the supply infrastructure of a private business model. Nevertheless, there are opportunities for more agency, as displayed in, for example, the ride-hailing app evolution in Nairobi, as well as the market opportunities for food vendors and urban gardeners in Cape Town.

The innovation that flows from digital interactions, I can confirm, is due not entirely to the availability of technology, but also to the imagination and sociocultural energies that motivate and infuse appropriation. It is informed by standing practices and histories. The three principles that inform the evolution of BebaBeba, for example, are local ownership, a simplified user experience and integration with local mobile money applications. The integration of Twiga into a supply chain of food sellers in Nairobi is a local understanding of the operations of *kibandas*, *dukas* and the needs of *mama mbongas*. The business model of Yebo Fresh's expansion is to understand local cookery trends and the strategies of *spaza shop* owners to deliver a product that is truly responsive to local markets and livelihoods. CANs' rapid expansion was as much a function of urgency during the early South African lockdown as a function of a value-driven framework that is respectful of local interests and needs. GoDown taps into a local imagination that uses culture as a vehicle to understand Nairobi's identity and thereby the collective imagination of its residents.

There is nevertheless a physical and infrastructural core to much of what I have discussed in this book, which speaks directly to the evolution of technology and digital power. The Twiga example is emblematic of the meeting of such power and socio-economic needs, with: M-Pesa and its ability to enable cashless exchange; the platform as a technical backbone that supports physical distribution functions; supply chain logistics that stretch beyond the usual formal markets and embrace street traders and other informal food vendors; data sourced through optimizing the IoT that enable modelling and future efficiency, and, of course, real-time management enabled through RFID tags attached to food crates. Analysed patterns can be used towards greater future efficiency and expansion. If the end result is greater coverage and inclusion, I believe that this is a hybrid that serves a socio-technical purpose of greater inclusivity and sustainability. Yebo Fresh's vision for future expansion includes enrolling local *spaza shops*, township fast-food restaurants, early childhood development centres, soup kitchens and associated charities into its platform network.

I also want to focus on the hybridity that typifies the combination of platforms in the business of civic activism and, more generally, in the operations of the SLURC and MapKibera, for example, the use of: video on YouTube; Twitter to keep supporters up to date; WhatsApp to summarize and brief the press; Facebook to organize; and Instagram to publicize. Variations on these functions and different combinations are employed to serve the purpose of the organization. Systems of working, or 'ways of working' in the language of CANs, inform the ways through which these technologies are combined, recombined and repurposed. Together with the offline forms of networking and connection, they form constellations that seek to influence popular opinion and policy, and thereby also guide further action. Furthermore, these hybrid constellations, both internally and externally, are deeply relational and dynamic, as tools, platforms and communication links are repurposed when the need arises. They also play a more substantive role in building identity through selective forms of representation. This is a deliberate terrain where the SLURC, MapKibera, NU and CANs are very clear about their outcomes. Yet, there have been shifts within the bounds of these intentions, some enabled or, at the very least, informed by digital platforms.

The addition of digital platforms to urban dynamics reveals an array of actors that span the public–private spectrum and the messiness in-between. Thus, another dimension of the hybrid city is the finely grained textures of the public–private interface. While much of the anxiety around the smart city is centred on corporate power in the public realm, what I believe the examples in this book show is that the separation of roles between the corporate sector and the state is not clear-cut at all and that both are implicated in the future making of cities, with overlaps in functions and assumed (and absconded) responsibilities. It also shows that civil society is alive and well, as well as able to forge partnerships with an array of actors, harnessing the ability of platforms to expand and enrol other functions. There is nevertheless a private sector sensibility at work, for example, in the expansion of the Twiga platform. Additions like M-Pesa functionality and access to credit are enabled through partnerships with financial institutions. Similarly, SafeBoda partnered with insurance companies to enable driver insurance for local vendors regarding cloud kitchens and food sales.

Finally, much like constellations in the solar system represent the past, present and future, so also do the disruptive practices captured here represent associations with traditions, legacies and future hopes. The contextual depth afforded by a situated approach reveals how urban life is sometimes not only 'rigged together from whatever is at hand' (Simone, 2011: 356), but also informed by 'what has worked and what has not'. In understanding a moment in time in contemporary urbanism, the temporal dimension emerges as an informant of how, why and what different socio-technical relations manifest.

The temporal is represented in the choice of technologies and the situated legacies in the cases discussed. CANs and CTT use both social media and more traditional forms of broadcast, such as radio and print media, to promote and mobilize their actions. The Sinani food voucher is a material manifestation of the hybrid nature of the network's ways of working; the financing is enabled through an online donation system using Snap Scan, a local mobile payment app, and credit card functions, and it is extended and organized through WhatsApp. In many ways, the voucher represents a hybrid quality of online and offline assistance. The advantages of using vouchers, as listed on the web site, include autonomy, discretion, health and safety. They can be customized to suit household needs and can be redeemed at supermarkets or local traders. This flexibility, enabled through technology, is specifically intended to support small local businesses. The use of video is frequent, and community television was also utilized. The legacies of activism and the learning from past experiences also inform how disruptive practice unfold and the strategies deployed to incorporate platforms, as can be seen with the CANs experience. Lessons from prior interventions and manifestations of epidemics like Ebola inform CANs and how the SLURC interacts with informal settlements. The 'slow burn' approach in activism, combined with technology-enabled quick responses in the activism of NU, is indicative of a push for a sustainable future and the continuous engagement with the present. The many languages of Afrofuturism engage a future that is constantly in dialogue with the past. Similarly, the knowledge-generation practices present in so many of these stories are expressions of agency through the definition of the present as a manifestation of past legacies and current regimes, and the framing of solutions towards more hopeful futures.

On disruption and hopeful futures

> Just as the actions in the present dictate the future, imagining the future can change the present. (Womack, 2013: 44)

Perhaps one of the big lessons that emerges from postcolonial STS is the associational ties that bind local practices to larger objectives as scientific ideas are appropriated and used towards broader ideological objectives, as also reflected in research elsewhere (Rajão and Duque, 2014). Platform-enabled disruptive practices make possible enlarged life worlds and imaginations, while also extending the public gaze to the invisible and marginalized. That in itself is a hopeful look towards the future. However, I do find my enthusiasm tempered by the following quotation from Abraham (2006: 210) when considering the inherent risks:

> To the extent that postcolonial techno-science may identify and address 'local' and incommensurable knowledges built around non-western ontologies, this formulation evokes the invisible knowledge work of subalterns being subsumed into capitalist property relations that will eventually lead to exploitation, expropriation and even extermination.

Certainly, some of the vignettes give some indication of the generation of a corporate or 'digital personhood' (Doherty, 2020) that creeps in. The disruption of established kinship practices, for example, can perhaps be interpreted as undermining local processes. However, public culture is a dynamic and evolving feature of urban life that weaves the past, present and future into its imagination. To place too much emphasis on the power of technology companies, for example, as usurpers of local traditions, is another form of technological determinism. It does not engage the embedded agency that guides the appropriation and remaking of digital platforms. The many respondents that I interviewed in the making of these vignettes and the people whose stories I engaged online are well aware of the power imbalances that impact the functioning and distribution of platforms, as well as their underlying technological and coded building blocks. There is an astute recognition of the structural imbalances and socio-spatial inequalities that impact the functioning of the spaces that engulf their everyday lives. Some of these actors may very well become (or have become) part of the neo-corporate conditions that define late capitalism. These are risks, of course, but my experience is that they do not negate the spaces created for engagement, creativity and activism. I believe that these vignettes show that the tenets and qualities of Afrofuturism, a form of expression that celebrates the African imagination while engaging its future, are here with us now in the present.

Notes

Introduction
1. See: www.oxfordlearnersdictionaries.com
2. See: www.wiego.org

Chapter 3
1. See: https://populationstat.com/
2. Ricky Thompson, personal communication, 26 February 2020.
3. Deepa Shekar, personal communication, 2 March 2020.
4. Not his real name.
5. Uber driver, personal communication, 23 October 2018.
6. See the BebaBeba web site, Facebook and Twitter pages.
7. Deepa Shekar, personal communication, 4 March 2020.
8. Ricky Thompson, Personal communication, 26 February 2020.
9. Deepa Shekar, personal communication, 4 March 2020.
10. Ricky Thompson, personal communication, 26 February 2020.
11. Ricky Thompson, personal communication, 26 February 2020.
12. Leka Tingitana, personal communication, 2 October 2018.

Chapter 4
1. Interview with Peter Njonjo, 20 April 2020. Available at: www.youtube.com/watch?v=702I2yD0VCg
2. See: https://techweez.com/2016/09/20/twiga-foods-grant-brooke-interview/
3. The HFIAS is based on a short questionnaire that examines households' behavioural and psychological manifestations of a lack of food access; examples include having to reduce the number of meals consumed or cut back on the quality of the food due to other spending priorities or lack of resources (see: https://inddex.nutrition.tufts.edu).
4. Interview with street trader in a Twiga promotional video. Available at: www.youtube.com/watch?v=iqQVAOZlFzQ
5. Interview with street trader in a Twiga promotional video. Available at: www.youtube.com/watch?v=iqQVAOZlFzQ
6. See: https://twiga.com/marketplace/
7. See: https://twiga.com/
8. See: https://twiga.com/
9. Gary Benatar, Personal communication, 27 May 2021.
10. See: www.yebofresh.co.za
11. Simon Peters, personal communication, 26 May 2021.

12. Gugulethu-Seaboard CAN, Facebook.
13. See: www.youtube.com/watch?v=wkSX-3PV6Cg
14. Dr Leanne Brady, personal communication, 15 September 2021.
15. See: https://roarmag.org/essays/cape-town-together-organizing-in-a-city-of-islands/
16. See: https://roarmag.org/essays/cape-town-together-organizing-in-a-city-of-islands/
17. Dr Leanne Brady, personal communication, 15 September 2021.
18. Dr Leanne Brady, personal communication, 15 September 2021.
19. Cape Talk Podcast, 'Lunch with Pippa Hudson', 6 April 2020.
20. 'Just start', video on the Gugulethu Urban Farming Initiative. Available at: https://seaboardcan.org/Gugulethu-Urban-Farming-Initiative
21. See: www.fao.org
22. See: www.youtube.com/watch?v=z69c8uTfIjA
23. See: www.youtube.com/watch?v=z69c8uTfIjA

Chapter 5

1. See: https://nu.org.za
2. I was an expert witness on the application, arguing the case that spatial apartheid had not been addressed by the City of Cape Town and the Western Cape Provincial Government.
3. See: https://nu.org.za/
4. 'Ndifuna Ukwazi' is an isiXhosa phrase loosely translated as 'I want to know'.
5. Kyla Hazell, Popular Education Officer, NU, personal communication, 5 October 2021.
6. Michael Clark, Head of Research and Advocacy, NU, personal communication, 5 October 2021.
7. Michael Clark, Head of Research and Advocacy, NU, personal communication, 5 October 2021.
8. Michael Clark, Head of Research and Advocacy, NU, personal communication, 5 October 2021.
9. Kyla Hazell, Popular Education Officer, NU, personal communication, 5 October 2021.
10. Kyla Hazell, Popular Education Officer, NU, personal communication, 5 October 2021.
11. Dr Leanne Brady, CTT, personal communication, 2 October 2021.
12. Confirmed by Brady, Hazell and Clark.
13. Dr Leanne Brady, CTT, personal communication, 2 October 2021.
14. Michael Clark, Head of Research and Advocacy, NU, personal communication, 5 October 2021.
15. See: https://sdinet.org/video/the-know-your-city-campaign/
16. 'Know Your City' flyer, distributed by the Cities Alliance and SDI. Available at: www.citiesalliance.org
17. I served on the SLURC's international advisory board from 2016 to 2019.
18. Joseph Macarthy, Director, SLURC, personal communication, 19 September 2021.
19. Software that enables live mapping by participants using their mobile phones.
20. Braima Koroma, Director of Research, SLURC, personal communication, 19 September 2021.
21. See: www.millefoto.com/unequalscenes
22. See: https://unequalscenes.com
23. See: https://unequalscenes.com/
24. Johnny Miller, African Drone, personal communication, 13 November 2018.
25. Johnny Miller, African Drone, personal communication, 13 November 2018.

NOTES

Chapter 6

1. See: https://chimurengachronic.co.za/the-internet-is-afropolitan/
2. See: https://digital.hbs.edu/platform-digit/submission/map-kibera-empowering-africas-biggest-slum-with-collective-wisdom/
3. Joshua Ogure, Project Coordinator, MapKibera Trust, personal communication, 30 May 2018.
4. See: www.intracen.org/news/Tech-Hubs-Critical-to-Africa-Covid-Recovery-Future-Growth-Learn-Ensure-Their-Own-Sustainability/
5. Jon Beardsley, Cloud Factory, Nairobi, personal communication, 2 March 2020; Baraka Mwau, local city planner, Nairobi, personal communication, 4 March 2020.
6. Jon Beardsley, Cloud Factory, Nairobi, personal communication, 2 March 2020; Baraka Mwau, local city planner, Nairobi, personal communication, 4 March 2020.
7. See: www.youtube.com/watch?v=y7xhQzJ0V8g
8. See: https://hbr.org/2019/01/the-era-of-move-fast-and-break-things-is-over
9. Joy Mboya, Nairobi, personal communication, March 2020.
10. See: www.youtube.com/watch?v=7Btpkn0dDr4
11. See: www.youtube.com/watch?v=ciDHH47UxEA
12. See: https://godowntransforms.org/2018/10/19/change-story-lincoln-maina/

Chapter 7

1. See: www.oxfordlearnersdictionaries.com

References

Abraham, I. (2006) The contradictory spaces of postcolonial techno-science. *Economic and Political Weekly*, 41(3), 210–17.

Achuka, V. (2018) Who will blink first between taxi drives and technology companies. *Standard Media*, 15 July. Available at: www.standardmedia.co.ke/business/article/2001288091/taxi-industry-s-uber-battle-just-gathering-speed

African Union (2018) *Drones on the Horizon: Transforming Africa's Agriculture*. Report of the High-Level African Union Panel on Emerging Technologies (APET) on Drones on the Horizon. NEPAD.

Afrilabs and Briter-Bridges (2019) Building a conducive setting for innovators to thrive: a qualitative and quantitative study of a hundred hubs across Africa. Available at: https://afrilabs.com/

Ajibade, I. (2017) Can a future city enhance urban resilience and sustainability? A political ecology analysis of Eko Atlantic city, Nigeria. *International Journal of Disaster Risk Reduction*, 26, 85–92.

Allagui, I. and Kuebler, J. (2011) The Arab Spring and the role of ICTs editorial introduction. *International Journal of Communication*, 5, 1435–42.

Anderson, B. and McFarlane, C. (2011) Assemblage and geography. *Area*, 43(2), 124–7.

Anderson, W. (2002) Introduction: postcolonial technoscience. *Social Studies of Science*, 32(5–6), 643–58.

Anderson, W. (2020) Postcolonial specters of STS. *East Asian Science, Technology and Society: An International Journal*, 11(2), 229–33.

Asenbaum, H. (2018) Cyborg activism: exploring the reconfigurations of democratic subjectivity in Anonymous. *New Media & Society*, 20(4), 1543–63.

Aurigi, A. and Odendaal, N. (2021) From 'smart in the box' to 'smart in the city': rethinking the socially sustainable smart city in context. *Journal of Urban Technology*, 28(1–2), 55–70.

Baptista, I. (2015) 'We live on estimates': everyday practices of prepaid electricity and the urban condition in Maputo, Mozambique. *International Journal of Urban and Regional Research*, 39(5), 1004–19.

Barns, S. (2019) *Platform Urbanism: Negotiating Platform Ecosystems in Connected Cities*. Cham: Springer.

Battersby, J. (2020) South Africa's lockdown regulations and the reinforcement of anti-informality bias. *Agriculture and Human Values*, 37(3), 543–4.

Battersby, J. and Crush, J. (2014) Africa's urban food deserts. *Urban Forum*, 25(2), 143–51.

Battersby, J. and Watson, V. (2018a) Addressing food security in African cities. *Nature Sustainability*, 1(4), 153–5.

Battersby, J. and Watson, V. (2018b) Introduction. In J. Battersby and V. Watson (eds) *Urban Food Systems Governance and Poverty in African Cities*. Abingdon: Routledge.

Baumann, K. (2018) Infrastructures of the imagination: building new worlds in media, art, & design. PhD Dissertation, University of Southern California.

Behrens, R., McCormick, D. and Mfinanga, D. (2015) *Paratransit in African Cities: Operations, Regulation and Reform*. Abingdon: Routledge.

Berney, R. (2011) Pedagogical urbanism: creating citizen space in Bogotá, Colombia. *Planning Theory*, 10(1), 16–34.

Bristow, T. (2012) We want the funk: what is Afrofuturism to the situation of digital arts in Africa? *Technoetic Arts*, 10(1), 25–32.

Burrell, J. (2012) *Invisible Users: Youth in the Internet Cafes of Urban Ghana*. Cambridge, MA: MIT Press.

Cardullo, P. (2020) *Citizens in the 'Smart City': Participation, Co-production, Governance*. Abingdon: Routledge.

Carrigan, M. and Fatsis, L. (2021) *The Public and Their Platforms: Public Sociology in an Era of Social Media*. Bristol: Policy Press.

Chakrabarty, D., Majumdar, R. and Sartori, A. (2007) *From the Colonial to the Postcolonial*. New Delhi: Oxford University Press.

Cheang, K.H. (2016) Exultant and cautionary imaginings at the interstices of architecture, technology and culture: an interview with Olalekan Jeyifous. *Science Fiction Studies*, 43(2), 419–23.

Cherlet, J. (2014) Epistemic and technological determinism in development aid. *Science, Technology, & Human Values*, 39(6), 773–94.

Civic Data Design Lab (2019) Urbanization and traffic in Nairobi. Available at: https://urbannext.net/urbanization-traffic-in-nairobi/

Cocola-Gant, A. and Gago, A. (2019) Airbnb, buy-to-let investment and tourism-driven displacement: a case study in Lisbon. *Environment and Planning A: Economy and Space*, 53(7). Available at: https://doi.org/10.1177%2F0308518X19869012

Corwin, J. E. (2018) 'Nothing is useless in nature': Delhi's repair economies and value-creation in an electronics 'waste' sector. *Environment and Planning A: Economy and Space*, 50(1), 14–30.

Cross, J. and Murray, D. (2018) The afterlives of solar power: waste and repair off the grid in Kenya. *Energy Research & Social Science*, 44, 100–9.

Crush, J. and Frayne, G.B. (2011) Urban food insecurity and the new international food security agenda. *Development Southern Africa*, 28(4), 527–44.

Crush, J. and Riley, L. (2018) Rural bias and urban food security. In J. Battersby and V. Watson (eds) *Urban Food Systems Governance and Poverty in African Cities*. Abingdon: Routledge, pp 42–55.

Crush, J., Frayne, B. and Pendleton, W. (2012) The crisis of food insecurity in African cities. *Journal of Hunger & Environmental Nutrition*, 7(2–3), 271–92.

CSM Association (2020) The mobile economy sub-Saharan Africa 2020. GSMA Intelligence. Available at: https://data.gsmaintelligence.com/research/research/research-2020/the-mobile-economy-sub-saharan-africa-2020

Danneels, E. (2004) Disruptive technology reconsidered: a critique and research agenda. *Journal of Product Innovation Management*, 21(4), 246–58.

Daramy, A. (2021) SLURC engages stakeholders. *Global Times News*, 20 June. Available at: www.facebook.com/globaltimesonline/posts/slurc-engages-stakeholders-by-lansana-fofanahthe-sierra-leone-urban-research-cen/2362652843863365/

Datta, A. (2015) New urban utopias of postcolonial India: 'entrepreneurial urbanization' in Dholera smart city, Gujarat. *Dialogues in Human Geography*, 5(1), 3–22.

Datta, A. (2018) The digital turn in postcolonial urbanism: smart citizenship in the making of India's 100 smart cities. *Transactions of the Institute of British Geographers*, 43(3), 405–19.

Deloitte & Touche (2015) Africa is ready to leapfrog the competition through smart cities technology. Available at: www2.deloitte.com/content/dam/Deloitte/za/Documents/risk/ZA_SMARTCITIESA4(VIEW)_020615.pdf

Dixon, T., Lannon, S. and Eames, M. (2018) Reflections on disruptive energy innovation in urban retrofitting: methodology, practice and policy. *Energy Research & Social Science*, 37, 255–9.

Doherty, J. (2017) Life (and limb) in the fast-lane: disposable people as infrastructure in Kampala's boda boda industry. *Critical African Studies*, 9(2), 192–209.

Doherty, J. (2020) Motorcycle taxis, personhood, and the moral landscape of mobility. *Geoforum*. Available at: https://doi.org/10.1016/j.geoforum.2020.04.003

Duminy, J., Odendaal, N. and Watson, V. (2014a) The education and research imperatives of urban planning professionals in Africa. In S. Parnell and E. Pieterse (eds) *Africa's Urban Revolution: Policy Pressures*. London: Zed Books Ltd, p 184.

Duminy, J., Odendaal, N. and Watson, V. (2014b) Case study research in Africa: methodological dimensions. In J. Duminy, J. Andreasen, F. Lerise, N. Odendaal and V. Watson (eds) *Planning and the Case Study Method in Africa*. Cham: Springer, pp 21–47.

Durodola, A. (2018) What the launch of BebaBeba could mean for Kenya's taxi industry. *Ventures Africa*, 20 September. Available at: http://venturesafrica.com/bebabeba-enters-kenyas-taxi-industry/

Easterling, K. (2014) *Extrastatecraft: The Power of Infrastructure Space*. London: Verso Books.

Esfandari, D.A. (2015) Gojek in conflict: cultural perspective. Paper presented at the International Conference on Transformation in Communication (ICOTIC).

Farías, I. and Bender, T. (2012) *Urban Assemblages: How Actor-Network Theory Changes Urban Studies*. Abingdon: Routledge.

Firmino, R., Cardoso, B. and Evangelista, R. (2019) Hyperconnectivity and (im)mobility: Uber and surveillance capitalism by the Global South. *Surveillance & Society*, 17(1/2): 205–12.

Fonjong, L. (2014) Rethinking the impact of structural adjustment programs on human rights violations in West Africa. *Perspectives on Global Development and Technology*, 13(1–2), 87–110.

Foth, M. (2006) Facilitating social networking in inner-city neighborhoods. *Computer*, 39(9), 44–50.

Foth, M. (2008) *Handbook of Research on Urban Informatics: The Practice and Promise of the Real-Time City*. Hershey: IGI Global.

Friederici, N. (2018) Hope and hype in Africa's digital economy: the rise of innovation hubs. In M. Graham (ed) *Digital Economies at Global Margins*. Boston, MA: MIT Press, pp 193–221.

Furlong, K. (2010) Small technologies, big change: rethinking infrastructure through STS and geography. *Progress in Human Geography*, 35(4), 460–82.

Furlong, K. (2014) STS beyond the 'modern infrastructure ideal': extending theory by engaging with infrastructure challenges in the South. *Technology in Society*, 38, 139–47.

Furlong, K. (2020) Geographies of infrastructure II: concrete, cloud and layered (in)visibilities. *Progress in Human Geography*, 45(1), 190–8.

Gerbaudo, P. (2012) *Tweets and the Streets: Social Media and Contemporary Activism*. London: Pluto Press.

Godard, X. (2008) Transport artisanal, esquisse de bilan pour la mobilité durable. Available at: www.researchgate.net/publication/228785986_Transport_artisanal_esquisse_de_bilan_pour_la_mobilite_durable

Goodfellow, T. and Titeca, K. (2012) Presidential intervention and the changing 'politics of survival' in Kampala's informal economy. *Cities*, 29(4), 264–70.

Graham, M. (2008) Warped geographies of development: the Internet and theories of economic development. *Geography Compass*, 2(3), 771–89.

Graham, M. (2020) Regulate, replicate, and resist: the conjunctural geographies of platform urbanism. *Urban Geography*, 41(3), 453–7.

Graham, S. and Marvin, S. (1996) *Telecommunications and the City* (vol 452). London: Routledge.

Graham, S. and Marvin, S. (2001) *Splintering Urbanism: Networked Infrastructures, Technological Mobilities and the Urban Condition*. Abingdon: Routledge.

Graham, S. and Thrift, N. (2007) Out of order: understanding repair and maintenance. *Theory, Culture & Society*, 24(3), 1–25.

Grebe, E. (2011) The treatment action campaign's struggle for AIDS treatment in South Africa: coalition-building through networks. *Journal of Southern African Studies*, 37(4), 849–68.

Guma, P.K. (2019) Smart urbanism? ICTs for water and electricity supply in Nairobi. *Urban Studies*, 56(11), 2333–52.

Guma, P.K. (2020) Incompleteness of urban infrastructures in transition: scenarios from the mobile age in Nairobi. *Social Studies of Science*, 50(5), 728–50.

Guma, P.K. and Monstadt, J. (2020) Smart city making? The spread of ICT-driven plans and infrastructures in Nairobi. *Urban Geography*, 42(3), 360–81.

Hagen, E. (2010) Putting Nairobi's slums on the map. *Development Outreach*, 12(1), 41–3.

Hagen, E. (2017) *Open Mapping from the Ground up: Learning from Map Kibera*, Making All Voices Count Research Report. Brighton: IDS.

Haraway, D. (1991) A cyborg manifesto: science, technology and socialist feminism in the late twentieth century. In D. Haraway (ed) *Simians, Cyborgs and Women: The Reinvention of Nature*. London: Free Association Books.

Harding, S. (2009) Postcolonial and feminist philosophies of science and technology: convergences and dissonances. *Postcolonial Studies*, 12(4), 401–21.

Harding, S. (2016) Latin American decolonial social studies of scientific knowledge. *Science, Technology, & Human Values*, 41(6), 1063–87.

Hayombe, P.O., Owino, F.O. and Awuor, F.O. (2018) Planning and governance of food systems in Kisumu City. In J. Battersby and V. Watson (eds) *Urban Food Systems Governance and Poverty in African Cities*. Abingdon: Routledge, pp 116–27.

Haythornthwaite, C. (2005) Social networks and Internet connectivity effects. *Information, Community & Society*, 8(2), 125–47.

Heeks, R. (2001) *Understanding E-Governance for Development*. Manchester: Institute for Development Policy and Management.

Howard, P.N. and Hussain, M.M. (2011) The upheavals in Egypt and Tunisia: the role of digital media. *Journal of Democracy*, 22(3), 35–48.

Howe, J. (2003) 'Filling the middle': Uganda's appropriate transport services. *Transport Reviews*, 23(2), 161–76.

Ibrahim, B. and Bize, A. (2018) Waiting together: the motorcycle taxi stand as Nairobi infrastructure. *Africa Today*, 65(2), 73–92.

Jaglin, S. (2008) Differentiating networked services in Cape Town: echoes of splintering urbanism? *Geoforum*, 39(6), 1897–906.

Jiménez, A. and Zheng, Y. (2021) Unpacking the multiple spaces of innovation hubs. *The Information Society*, 37(3), 163–76.

Joubert, L., Battersby, J. and Watson, V. (2018) Tomatoes and taxi ranks: running our cities to fill the food gaps. African Centre for Cities, University of Cape Town, South Africa.

Kahende, K. (2020) Little launches ambulance services. Little blog, 30 May. Available at: www.little.bz/blog/little-launches-emergency-ambulance-services/

Kaika, M. (2017) 'Don't call me resilient again!': the new urban agenda as immunology … or … what happens when communities refuse to be vaccinated with 'smart cities' and indicators. *Environment and Urbanization*, 29(1), 89–102.

Kellogg, S. (2016) Digitizing dissent: cyborg politics and fluid networks in contemporary Cuban activism. *Teknokultura*, 13(1), 19–53.

Kitchin, R. and McArdle, G. (2016) What makes big data, big data? Exploring the ontological characteristics of 26 datasets. *Big Data & Society*. Available at: https://doi.org/2053951716631130

Kitchin, R., Lauriault, T.P. and McArdle, G. (2015) Knowing and governing cities through urban indicators, city benchmarking and real-time dashboards. *Regional Studies, Regional Science*, 2(1), 6–28.

Konadu-Agyemang, K. (2000) The best of times and the worst of times: structural adjustment programs and uneven development in Africa: the case of Ghana. *The Professional Geographer*, 52(3), 469–83.

Krishnan, A., Banga, K. and Mendez-Parra, M. (2020) Disruptive technologies in agricultural value chains. *Insights from East Africa*. Working paper 576.

Lawhon, M., Ernstson, H. and Silver, J. (2014) Provincializing urban political ecology: towards a situated UPE through African urbanism. *Antipode*, 46(2), 497–516.

Lawhon, M., Nilsson, D., Silver, J., Ernstson, H. and Lwasa, S. (2018) Thinking through heterogeneous infrastructure configurations. *Urban Studies*, 55(4), 720–32.

Lewis, C. (2005) Negotiating the net: the Internet in South Africa (1990–2003). *Information Technologies and International Development*, 2(3), 1–28.

Ling, R. and Horst, H.A. (2011) Mobile communication in the Global South. *New Media & Society*, 13(3), 363–74.

Lockhart, A., While, A., Marvin, S. et al (2021) Making space for drones: the contested reregulation of airspace in Tanzania and Rwanda. *Transactions of the Institute of British Geographers*, 46(4), 850–65.

Madon, S. (2004) Evaluating the developmental impact of e-governance initiatives: an exploratory framework. *The Electronic Journal of Information Systems in Developing Countries*, 20(1), 1–13.

Madon, S., Reinhard, N., Roode, D. and Walsham, G. (2010) Digital inclusion projects in developing countries: processes of institutionalization. *Information Technology for Development*, 15(2), 95–107.

Marvin, S. and Luque-Ayala, A. (2017) Urban operating systems: diagramming the city. *International Journal of Urban and Regional Research*, 41(1), 84–103.

Marvin, S., Luque-Ayala, A. and McFarlane, C. (2015) *Smart Urbanism: Utopian Vision or False Dawn?* Abingdon: Routledge.

Mattern, S. (2018) Maintenance and care. *Places Journal*, 20 November. Available at: https://placesjournal.org/article/maintenance-and-care/?cn-reloaded=1

McCann, E., Roy, A. and Ward, K. (2013) Assembling/worlding cities. *Urban Geography*, 34(5), 581–9.

McFarlane, C. and Söderström, O. (2017) On alternative smart cities: from a technology-intensive to a knowledge-intensive smart urbanism. *City*, 21(3–4): 312–28.

Mitchell, H. and Odendaal, N. (2015) From the fringes: South Africa's smart township citizens. In M. Foth, M. Brynskov and T. Ojala (eds) *Citizen's Right to the Digital City*. Cham: Springer, pp 137–159.

Mitchell, W.J. (1996) *City of Bits: Space, Place, and the Infobahn*. Cambridge, MA: MIT Press.

Moodley, S. (2005) The promise of e-development? A critical assessment of the state ICT for poverty reduction discourse in South Africa. *Perspectives on Global Development and Technology*, 4(1), 1–26.

Mutiso, W. and Behrens, R. (2011) 'Boda boda' bicycle taxis and their role in urban transport systems: case studies of Kisumu and Nakura, Kenya. Available at: http://repository.up.ac.za/handle/2263/17308

Myers, G. (2015) A world-class city-region? Envisioning the Nairobi of 2030. *American Behavioral Scientist*, 59(3), 328–46.

Odendaal, N. (2011) Splintering urbanism or split agendas? Examining the spatial distribution of technology access in relation to ICT policy in Durban, South Africa. *Urban Studies*, 48(11), 2375–97.

Odendaal, N. (2014) Space matters: the relational power of mobile technologies. *Urbe: Revista Brasileira de Gestão Urbana*, 6(1), 31–45.

Odendaal, N. (2018) Smart innovation at the margins: learning from Cape Town and Kibera. In A. Karvonen, F. Cugurullo and F. Caprotti (eds) *Inside Smart Cities*. Abingdon: Routledge, pp 243–57.

Odendaal, N. (2019) Appropriating 'big data': exploring the emancipatory potential of the data strategies of civil society organizations in Cape Town, South Africa. In P. Cardullo, C. Di Feliciantonio and R. Kitchin (eds) *The Right to the Smart City*. Bingley: Emerald Publishing Limited.

Odendaal, N. (2020) Everyday urbanisms and the importance of place: exploring the elements of the emancipatory smart city. *Urban Studies*, 58(3), 639–54.

Odendaal, N. (2021a) Constructing an 'infrastructure of care': understanding the institutional remnants and socio-technical practices that constitute South Africa's Covid-19 response. *Urban Geography*, 42(3), 391–8.

Odendaal, N. (2021b) Platform urbanism and hybrid places in African cities. In A. Aurigi and N. Odendaal (eds) *Shaping Smart for Better Cities*. Amsterdam: Elsevier, pp 203–19.

Odendaal, N. (2022) Splintering by proxy: a reflection on the spatial impacts and distributed agency of platform urbanism. *Journal of Urban Technology*, 29(1), 21–7.

Odendaal, N. and McCann, A. (2016) Spatial planning in the Global South: reflections on the Cape Town spatial development framework. *International Development Planning Review*, 38(4), 405.

Okarofor, N. (2010) The go-slow. In J.J. Adams (ed) *The Way of the Wizard*. Athens: Prime Press.

Parnell, S. and Pieterse, D.E. (2014) *Africa's Urban Revolution*. London: Bloomsbury Publishing.

Pieterse, E. (2014) Epistemological practices of southern urbanism. Paper to be presented at the ACC Academic Seminar, 21 February.

Philip, K., Irani, L. and Dourish, P. (2012) Postcolonial computing: a tactical survey. *Science, Technology, & Human Values*, 37(1), 3–29.

Pink, S. (2009) Situating sensory ethnography: from academia to intervention. In S. Pink (ed) *Doing Sensory Ethnography*. Thousand Oaks, CA: Sage Publications, pp 7–23.

Pink, S. (2016) Digital ethnography. In S. Kubitschko and A. Kaun (eds) *Innovative Methods in Media and Communication Research*. London: Palgrave Macmillan, pp 161–5.

Pink, S. and Morgan, J. (2013) Short-term ethnography: intense routes to knowing. *Symbolic Interaction*, 36(3), 351–61.

Pink, S., Ardèvol, E. and Lanzeni, D. (2020) Digital materiality. In S. Pink, E. Ardèvol and D. Lanzeni (eds) *Digital Materialities*. Abingdon: Routledge, pp 1–26.

Plantin, J.-C., Lagoze, C., Edwards, P.N. and Sandvig, C. (2016) Infrastructure studies meet platform studies in the age of Google and Facebook. *New Media & Society*, 20(1), 293–310.

Pollio, A. (2019) Forefronts of the sharing economy: Uber in Cape Town. *International Journal of Urban and Regional Research*, 43(4), 760–75.

Pollio, A. (2020) Making the Silicon Cape of Africa: tales, theories and the narration of startup urbanism. *Urban Studies*, 57(13), 2715–32.

Potts, D. (2009) The slowing of sub-Saharan Africa's urbanization: evidence and implications for urban livelihoods. *Environment and Urbanization*, 21(1), 253–9.

Rajão, R. and Duque, R.B. (2014) Between purity and hybridity: technoscientific and ethnic myths of Brazil. *Science, Technology, & Human Values*, 39(6), 844–74.

Rigon, A., Macarthy, J., Koroma, B., Walker, J. and Frediani, A.A. (2017) Partnering with higher education institutions for social and environmental justice in the Global South: lessons from the Sierra Leone Urban Research Centre. *DPU News*, 62, 2–5.

Robins, S. (2014a) The 2011 toilet wars in South Africa: justice and transition between the exceptional and the everyday after apartheid. *Development and Change*, 45(3), 479–501.

Robins, S. (2014b) Slow activism in fast times: reflections on the politics of media spectacles after apartheid. *Journal of Southern African Studies*, 40(1), 91–110.

Rodgers, S. and Moore, S. (2020) Platform phenomenologies: social media as experiential infrastructures of urban public life. In M. Hodson, J. Kasmire, A. McMeekin, J. Stehlin and K. Ward (eds) *Urban Platforms and the Future City*. Abingdon: Routledge, pp 209–22.

Roever, S. and Skinner, C. (2016) Street vendors and cities. *Environment and Urbanization*, 28(2), 359–74.

Rosenberg, L. and Brent, A. (2020) Infrastructure disruption in 'Silicon Savannah': exploring the idea of the creative class and their relation to quality of place in Nairobi, Kenya. *International Journal of Urban and Regional Research*, 44(5), 809–20.

Roy, A., Zalzala, A.M. and Kumar, A. (2016) Disruption of things: a model to facilitate adoption of IoT-based innovations by the urban poor. *Procedia Engineering*, 159, 199–209.

Sadowski, J. (2020a) Cyberspace and cityscapes: on the emergence of platform urbanism. *Urban Geography*, 41(3), 448–52.

Sadowski, J. (2020b) The internet of landlords: digital platforms and new mechanisms of rentier capitalism. *Antipode*, 52(2), 562–80.

Salaudeen, S. (2020) 'A rushed decision': angry commuters disapprove of controversial Lagos Okada ban. *CNN*, 14 February. Available at: https://edition.cnn.com/2020/02/14/africa/lagos-okada-keke-ban/index.html

Schech, S. (2002) Wired for change: the links between ICTs and development discourses. *Journal of International Development: The Journal of the Development Studies Association*, 14(1), 13–23.

Shin, D.-H. (2009) Ubiquitous city: urban technologies, urban infrastructure and urban informatics. *Journal of Information Science*, 35(5), 515–26.

REFERENCES

Sibanda, L. and von Blottnitz, H. (2018) Food value chains in Kisumu, Kitwe, and Epworth: environmental and social hotspots. In J. Batterby and V. Watson (eds) *Urban Food Systems Governance and Poverty in African Cities*. Abingdon: Routledge, pp 169–81.

Simone, A. (2004) People as infrastructure: intersecting fragments in Johannesburg. *Public Culture*, 16(3), 407–29.

Simone, A. (2010) Infrastructure, real economies, and social transformation: assembling the components for regional urban development in Africa. In E. Pieterse (ed) *Urbanization Imperatives for Africa: Transcending Policy Inertia*. Cape Town: African Centre for Cities, pp 24–36.

Simone, A. (2011) The ineligible majority: urbanizing the postcolony in Africa and Southeast Asia. *Geoforum*, 42(3), 266–70.

Simone, A. and Pieterse, E. (2017) *New Urban Worlds: Inhabiting Dissonant Times*. Hoboken, NJ: John Wiley & Sons.

Smit, W. (2016) Urban governance and urban food systems in Africa: examining the linkages. *Cities*, 58, 80–6.

Söderström, O. and Mermet, A.-C. (2020) When Airbnb sits in the control room: platform urbanism as actually existing smart urbanism in Reykjavík. *Frontiers in Sustainable Cities*. Available at: https://doi.org/10.3389/frsc.2020.00015

Söderström, O., Blake, E. and Odendaal, N. (2021) More-than-local, more-than-mobile: the smart city effect in South Africa. *Geoforum*, 122, 103–17.

South African Urban Food and Farming Trust (2020) *Food Dialogues Report 2020*. Available at: https://capetown.fooddialogues.info/

Stehlin, J., Hodson, M. and McMeekin, A. (2020) Platform mobilities and the production of urban space: toward a typology of platformization trajectories. *Environment and Planning A: Economy and Space*, 52(7), 1250–68.

Steyn, N.P., McHiza, Z., Hill, J. et al (2014) Nutritional contribution of street foods to the diet of people in developing countries: a systematic review. *Public Health Nutrition*, 17(6), 1363–74.

Summerton, J (1994) Introductory essay: the systems approach to technological change. In J. Summerton (ed.) *Changing Large Technical Systems*. Boulder, CO: Westview Press, pp 1–21.

Toivonen, T. and Friederici, N. (2015) Time to define what a 'hub' really is. *Stanford Social Innovation Review*. Available at: https://doi.org/10.48558/N1BD-8S82

Toriro, P. (2018) Urban food production in Harare, Zimbabwe. In J. Batterby and V. Watson (eds) *Urban Food Systems Governance and Poverty in African Cities*. Abingdon: Routledge, pp 154–66.

Tostensen, A., Tvedten, I. and Vaa, M. (2001) The urban crisis, governance and associational life. In T. Tostensen, I. Tvedten and M. Vaa (eds) *Associational Life in African Cities: Popular Responses to the Urban Crisis*. Uppsala: Nordic Africa Institute, pp 7–26.

Townsend, A.M. (2013) *Smart Cities: Big Data, Civic Hackers, and the Quest for a New Utopia*. New York: W.W. Norton & Company.

Turok, I. and Watson, V. (2001) Divergent development in South African cities: strategic challenges facing Cape Town. *Urban Forum*, 12(2), 119–38.

UNDESA (United Nations, Department of Economic and Social Affairs) (2019) *World Urbanization Prospects: The 2018 Revision*. New York, NY: United Nations.

UNDP (United Nations Development Programme) (2017) *Income Inequality Trends in Sub-Saharan Africa: Divergence, Determinants and Consequences*. New York, NY: United Nations.

Van Doorn, N. (2019) A new institution on the block: on platform urbanism and Airbnb citizenship. *New Media & Society*, 22(10), 1808–26.

Van Ryneveld, M., Whyle, E. and Brady, L. (2022) What is COVID-19 teaching us about community health systems? A reflection from a rapid community-led mutual aid response in Cape town, South Africa. *International Journal of Health Policy and Management*, 11(1), 5–8.

Vergès, F. (2017) Digital Africa. *Journal of the African Literature Association*, 11(1), 45–9.

Wainaina, E. (2016) What next for small players in Kenya's taxi hailing business? *Techweez*, 13 July. Available at: https://techweez.com/2016/07/13/kenyas-taxi-hailing-business-small-players-future/

Warf, B. (1995) Telecommunications and the changing geographies of knowledge transmission in the late 20th century. *Urban Studies*, 32(2), 361–78.

Watson, V. (2013) African urban fantasies: dreams or nightmares? *Environment and Urbanization*, 26(1), 215–31.

Watson, V. (2015) The allure of 'smart city' rhetoric: India and Africa. *Dialogues in Human Geography*, 5(1), 36–9.

Wellman, B., Haase, A.Q., Witte, J. and Hampton, K. (2001) Does the Internet increase, decrease, or supplement social capital? Social networks, participation, and community commitment. *American Behavioral Scientist*, 45(3), 436–55.

Wiig, A. and Masucci, M. (2020) Digital infrastructures, services, and spaces. In M. Hodson, J. Kasmire, A. McMeekin, J.G. Stehlin and K. Ward (eds) *Urban Platforms and the Future City: Transformations in Infrastructure, Governance, Knowledge and Everyday Life*. Abingdon: Routledge, p 70.

Willis, K.S. and Aurigi, A. (2017) *Digital and Smart Cities*. Abingdon: Routledge.

Wilson, J., Garay-Tamajon, L. and Morales-Perez, S. (2022) Politicising platform-mediated tourism rentals in the digital sphere: Airbnb in Madrid and Barcelona. *Journal of Sustainable Tourism*, 30(5), 1080–101.

Womack, Y.L. (2013) *Afrofuturism: The World of Black Sci-fi and Fantasy Culture*. Chicago: Chicago Review Press.

Index

References to figures appear in *italic* type. References to endnotes show both the page number and the note number (231n3).

4G 7
4IR *see* Fourth Industrial Revolution
9/11 107

A
Accra 5, 53, 104
activism 10, 13, 14, 19, 21, 51, 60, 69, 70–9, 81–3, 85–7, 90, 94, 98, 99, 109, 110, 118–26
actor–network theory (ANT) 30
advertising 101
advocacy 14, 23, 36, 71, 74, 81, 92, 94, 116, 118
African Centre for Cities 59, 98
African Food Security Urban Network (AFSUN) 51
African Union 66
Afrofuturism 15, 89, 90, 99, 100, 104, 105, 114, 121, 125, 126
agriculture 13, 51, 53, 65–6
 see also farming
Airbnb 3, 13, 19, 26, 45, 75
air quality 23
algorithm 18, 20, 27, 42, 57, 70–3, 77, 104
ambulance 42–3
Android 7
apartheid 12, 58, 60, 62, 69, 70, 72, 74, 75, 86, 120, 128n2
 see also segregation
application programming interface (API) 22, 23, 27
appropriation 2, 4, 6, 8, 10, 14, 18, 20, 26, 28, 32, 35, 40, 47, 48, 72, 75, 76, 85, 88, 89, 101, 105, 106, 109, 122, 125
Arab Spring 71
architecture 3, 30, 56, 79, 101, 114–15
artefact 7, 29, 62, 89, 116
artificial intelligence (AI) 6, 65
arts centre 15, 89, 97
autonomy 11, 60, 63, 67, 115, 124

B
bananas 49–51, 54, 114
banking 44, 45, 55, 56, 58
Barcelona 21
BebaBeba 11, 35, 41–3, 123, 127n6
big data 20, 70, 73
biology 77
blackness 99–100
boda-boda 11, 24, 33, 36, *37*, 38, *39*, 43, 46–8, 82, 90, 111, 112, 116, 119
 see also SafeBoda
Bolt 40
Brazil 34–5
Burkina Faso 52
Butler, Octavia 99, 100
bypass 40, 111

C
Cape Town 1, 4, 11–13, 21, 26, 35, 39, 42, 44, 50, 52, 59, 60, *64*, 68, 72–4, 79, *84*, 85, 90, 97, 99, 108, 112, 113, 115, 118–22, 128n2
Cape Town Together (CTT) 12, 50, 60, 73, 76, 77, 79, 80, 85, 115, 116, 118, 122, 124
capitalism 25, 35, 43, 101, 109, 125, 126
Central Business District (CBD) 62, 74
Centre of Dialogue on Human Settlement and Poverty Alleviation (CODOHSAPA) 82
charity 12, 68, 123
chief executive officer (CEO) 49, 56, 60
chief operations officer (COO) 33, 37
children 52, 57, 102, 103, 123
Chimurenga magazine 88
China 7, 53
citizenship 18, 21, 28, 90–1, 98, 104, 118
cityscape 104
civil society organization (CSO) 19, 57, 60, 68, 73, 81, 82, 91

141

climate change 4, 5, 12, 48–9, 65–7, 113
    see also global warming
Cloud Factory 129n5, 129n6
CNN 49
Colombia 73, 81
Comic Relief 82
community action network (CAN) 12–13, 59, 61, 62, 63, 64–5, 68–9, 72, 113, 115, 117, 120, 128n12
community group 25, 73
community kitchen 12, 61
conjectural geographies 26
constellation 47, 109, 120–4
cooperative 4, 11, 26, 34, 38, 117
corporate social responsibility (CSR) 43
COVID-19 4, 6, 9, 11, 12, 24, 42, 48, 48, 50, 55, 57–61, 82, 83, 90, 91, 96, 97, 110, 115, 119
    see also lockdown
creativity 32, 64, 96, 99, 105, 126
crime 25, 92
Cuba 79–80, 86
cyberculture 100
cybersecurity 81
cyberspace 28, 105
cyborg 13, 14, 70–83, 85–7, 109, 118

D
Datta, Ayona 7, 18
death 102–3
democracy 70–2, 106
determinism 6, 95, 106–7, 125
diabetes 60
diaspora 99–100
digital
    communities 17
    engagement 100
    personhood 56, 125
    platform 2, 3, 5, 10, 12, 15, 16, 19–22, 24–6, 30, 39, 50, 54, 58–61, 62, 65, 71, 73, 76, 82, 98, 105, 108–10, 112–14, 119–25
    realm 40, 89, 90, 97, 105, 122
    revolution 34, 100
disease 60, 65
    see also Ebola, diabetes, obesity
disruption 2–4, 10, 11, 13, 16, 21, 24, 27, 34–5, 39, 40, 43, 45–8, 55–6, 108–9, 125
dissensus 70–1, 85, 118
diversity 1, 9, 12, 13, 19, 25, 27, 28, 53, 62, 100, 113, 115
Drivers and Partners Association of Kenya (DPAK) 41
drone 13, 14, 30, 46, 66–9, 73, 83–4, 111, 113, 116–20, 128n24, 128n25
    photography 14, 73, 83, 84, 120
Dubai 1, 5, 6, 100, 101
dukas 54, 56, 58, 68, 113, 123
Durban 20, 53
dystopia 101, 105

E
East Africa 4, 30, 33, 38, 56, 66, 92, 94, 109
Ebola 60, 110, 125
e-commerce 65
Economist, The 83
ecosystem 5, 7, 10, 11, 14, 55, 62, 66, 68, 90, 97, 98
e-governance 18
Egypt 71
electricity 6, 20, 27, 62, 96, 104, 114
embeddedness 2, 47
employment 9, 24, 26, 31, 39, 57, 74, 96
empowerment 13, 20, 28, 34, 44, 69, 94, 96
entrepreneur 5, 35, 41, 95, 96, 97, 114
ethics 18
exploitation 34, 35, 119, 122, 125

F
Facebook 62, 77, 79, 107, 113, 123, 127n6, 128n12ch4
famine 110
fantasy 1, 17, 18, 99, 109
farming 12, 51, 54, 55, 59, 61, 64, 65–6, 119, 128n20
    see also agriculture, Gugulethu Urban Farming Initiative (GUFI)
Federation of the Urban Poor (FEDUP) 82
Fees must Fall 60, 120
festival 83, 98, 99
fiction 14, 15, 99
    see also science fiction
financial institution 41, 55, 124
flooding 65
fog computing 23
food 10, 11, 24, 37, 51–4, 55, 57–8, 60–2, 65–70, 90, 91, 102, 110–13, 118, 119, 123, 127n3
    crisis 49, 57, 60
    fast 52, 123
    grower 61, 111
    industry 67
    market 112
    poverty 59–60
    relief 62
    safety 53
    security 10, 12–13, 48, 51–3, 57, 59, 64–6, 68, 90, 108, 113
    value chain 12, 49, 50, 56, 60–6, 113, 114, 115
    see also hunger
Food and Agriculture Organisation (FAO) 51, 128n21
Food Dialogues, The 49, 59
formalization 16, 24, 37, 119
Fourth Industrial Revolution (4IR) 5
Freetown 14, 82, 86, 108, 113, 117, 118, 120
fruit and vegetables 48, 49, 51, 53, 54
    see also bananas

INDEX

G
gardening 5, 12, 13, 50, 63, 64, 68, 99, 120–2
gender 67, 113
gentrification 13, 21, 74–6, 86
geospatial dimensions 16, 43
Ghana 52, 104
Global North 10, 21, 34
Global Positioning System (GPS) 36, 58, 103, 107
Global South 10, 16–18, 21, 24, 32, 34, 82, 103, 109, 119
Global System for Mobile Communications Association (GSMA) 6, 7
global warming 49
see also climate change
GoDown 15, 89, 97–100, 105, 115, 121, 123
go-slow 100–3
governance 3, 4, 12, 13, 16, 18, 20–8, 39, 51, 53, 66, 70–2, 91, 108, 110, 111, 116, 118
Graham, Mark 26
see also conjectural geographies
gross domestic product (GDP) 66
Guatemala 49
Gugulethu Urban Farming Initiative (GUFI) 64, 128n20

H
hackathons 23, 96
hacking 10, 25, 33–9, 42
Haraway, Donna 14
harvest 54
healthcare 4
see also hospital
heterogeneity 19, 21, 23, 25, 29, 31, 46, 71, 80, 86, 95
homelessness 112, 116, 120
hospital 37, 56, 61, 75, 92
Household Food Insecurity Access Scale (HFIAS) 51, 127n3
housing 8, 13, 21, 24, 73–8, 91, 110, 117
see also property
human–computer interaction 4
hunger 4, 51, 115

I
Ibadan 44, 45
IBM 19
iHub 15, 94, 95, 98, 109
income 3, 9, 11, 13, 34, 36–8, 41, 48, 51–6, 59, 60, 62, 68, 73–4, 112, 115
India 18, 64
inequality 9, 13, 16, 20, 25, 34, 48, 72, 73, 83–5, 113, 118
information and communication technology (ICT) 1, 5, 8, 18–20, 44, 65, 70, 71, 94, 95, 106
for development (ICT4D) 18, 28, 106

information dissemination 19, 72, 83
infrastructure 1–10, 18, 28–32, 39, 40, 43, 45, 47, 49–53, 58, 62, 68, 72, 83, 90, 95–9, 101–5, 106, 110, 112–16, 122
innovation 1–4, 8, 16, 17, 19, 20, 22, 24, 30, 32, 40–6, 67, 84, 91, 95, 98, 103–8, 114, 117, 122
hub 4, 84, 89, 91, 95, 105, 114
Instagram 77, 78, 79, 123
insurance 37, 41, 56, 115, 124
Internet of Things (IoT) 4, 20, 34, 57, 107, 123
investment 1, 5, 7, 20, 21, 28, 31, 50, 51, 94, 103, 112, 122
isiXhosa 128n4

J
Jewish community 76
Jeyifous, Olalekani 101–3
journalism 77, 79, 84

K
Kampala 11, 33, 36, 37, *39*, 43–5, 47, 90, 108, 111, 116, 119, 120
City Capital Authority (KCCA) 33
Kenya 2, 5, 7, 11, 12, 19, 27, 32–4, 38, 40–5, 49, 51–4, 57, 58, 89, 92, 95, 96, 99, 104, 113, 115, 119
see also Vision 2030
kibandas 5, 54, 68, 123
Kibera 15, 19, 40, *55*, 89, 91, 92, *93*, 94, 105, 107, 110, 113, 118, 124
security map *93*
see also MapKibera
kinship 40, 71, 90, 103, 111, 119, 125
knowledge and technology 106–7
Know Your City 14, 73, 81–3, 91, 92, 128n15, 128n16
Konza Tech City 5, 95, 97

L
labour 11, 14, 21, 34, 35, 39, 42, 76, 104, 119
Lagos 5, 45, 83, 101–2
Lake Victoria Challenge 84
leapfrogging 3, 7, 106, 112
livelihood 1, 2, 4, 6, 9, 11, 13, 17, 18, 24, 25, 28, 31–9, 43–53, 58, 60, 65–70, 82, 90, 95, 103, 106, 110, 112–17, 121, 123
live mapping 43, 128n19
loan 55–6
lobbying 45, 116, 117
local government 9, 23, 38, 81, 82
lockdown 6, 9, 12, 50, 55, 57, 59–62, 82, 90, 113, 117, 119, 123
Los Angeles 89
Lyft 11, 40

M
macroeconomic 4, 28, 44
Mali 52

mama mbongas 54, 68, 90, 113, 123
MapKibera 15, 19, 40, 89, 91–4, 105, 107, 110, 114, 118, 123, 124, 129n3
marginalization 11, 13, 57, 59, 60, 68, 93, 101, 113, 125
Massachusetts Institute of Technology (MIT) 107
matatus 33
Mbembe, Achille 88
megastructure 101
middle class 44, 58
Miller, Johnny 83, *84*, 120, 128n24, 128n25
  see also Unequal Scenes
Mitchell, William 18
mobile phone 1, 6, 7, 36, 58, 62, 63, 82, 92, 101–4, 116, 128n19
mobility 10–11, 26, 31, 32–9, 43, 45–50, 84, 108, 110, 117–19, 122
mobilization 13–15, 19, 27, 28, 42, 51, 52, 60, 61, 68–72, 74, 76, 77, 80, 81, 85, 87, 90, 91, 108, 112, 120
modelling 20, 123
modernism 3, 6, 28, 29, 114
money 15, 40–5, 55, 123
motorcycle 11, 24, 33, 36, 45, 102, 111, 112
Mozambique 27
M-Pesa 40, 45, 55, 57, 58, 68, 97, 107, 115, 123, 124
multi-actor collaboration 24
multinational companies (MNCs) 3, 5, 7, 8, 10, 100
municipalism 19
Museum of Contemporary Art Africa (MOCAA) 75
Muslim 13, 67
mythology 102–5, 114, 121

N

Nairobi 4–6, 11, 12, 15, 19, 25, 35, 40–4, 47, 48, 49, 54, *55*, 89–98, 108, 109, 112, 115, 120–3, 129n5, 129n6, 129n9
  see also Twiga
Narrative Initiative, The 84
National Bureau of Statistics 67
nationhood 18
Ndifuna Ukwazi (NU) 13, 14, 78, 128n4
neoliberalism 2, 18, 19, 96
networking 15, 18, 46, 62, 73, 80, 95–8, 105, 112, 115, 116, 123
Nigeria 2, 44, 45, 52, 102, 122
  see also Ibadan
Njonjo, Peter 49, 127n1ch4
non-governmental organization (NGO) 12, 57, 92, 96
nutrition 12, 48, 50–3, 60, 112

O

obesity 60
OpenStreetMap 92

outreach 50, 62, 71, 105
ownership 6, 41, 94, 97, 117, 123

P

pandemic *see* COVID-19
paratransit 11, 33, 39, 82, 91, 111, 117, 122
personhood 40, 56, 125
Philadelphia 26
photography 14, 73, 83, 84, 120, 121
place making 14, 25, 39, 105, 110, 114, 121
platform economy 3, 12, 16, 19, 21, 28, 34, 39, 43, 94, 95
police 36, 61, 92
policymaker 14, 25, 51, 73, 110, 120
political ecology 21, 28
politician 74, 120
polling station 92
population 6, 8, 9, 11, 33, 49, 50, 60, 66, 72, 99, 103
postcolonialism 10, 14–20, 29, 31, 35, 46, 102, 103, 108, 121, 125
post-industrial 28
poverty 1, 8, 13, 28, 51, 59, 60, 73, 82, 85
power 3, 5, 13, 14, 19, 20–3, 28–31, 44, 46, 47, 65, 69, 70, 80–6, 88, 89, 94, 96, 99, 109, 112, 116, 118, 120–6
private investment 20, 28, 51
problem solving 4, 10, 17, 19, 27, 31, 69, 70, 104, 109, 120
professionalism 37, 46, 111, 119
property 5, 7, 13, 26, 73–6, 80, 125
  see also housing
protein 52
provincialization 29
public good 113, 120
public health 52, 59, 60, 85
publicity 19, 72
public sphere 23, 90
public transport 9, 11, 24, 74, 112
Pul Slum Pan People (PSPP) 82

Q

Quick Paint 102

R

race 73, 99, 100
radio frequency identification (RFID) 57, 123
Ramblr 82
Reclaim the City (RtC) 74, 75, 76, 80
recycling 101, 114
regulation 16, 23, 25–7, 46, 106, 110–19
Relog 56–7, 116
ResiliArt 97
retail 50–4, 56, 68
ride-hailing 11, 34, 35, 40, 41, 45, 47, 109, 112, 122
rideshare 43, 45, 48
road safety 24, 46, 111

INDEX

S

SafeBoda 11, 24, 33–9, 43–8, 56, 88, 90, 111, 115, 116, 119, 120, 122, 124
see also boda-boda
safety 19, 24, 36, 37, 45, 46, 53, 63, 68, 81, 84, 111, 116, 124
sanitation 9, 51, 53, 59, 85
saturation 26, 34
school 57, 60, 74, 94, 99, 103
science and technology studies (STS) 2, 10, 14–16, 18, 20, 21, 28–32, 35, 100, 106–9, 125
science fiction 15, 99
Sea Point 62, 74, 76
segregation 73, 101, 117, 120
see also apartheid
Sendy 11, 44
Shack/ Slum Dwellers International (SDI) 14, 73, 81, 83, 91–3, 114, 128n15, 128n16
ShareCab 40, 41, 73
Shekar, Deepa 37, 43, 44, 127n3, 127n7, 127n9
Sierra Leone 2, 14, 73, 115, 118
  Urban Research Centre (SLURC) 14, 82, 83, 91, 93, 110, 117, 122–5, 128n17, 128n18, 128n20
  see also Freetown
Silicon Savannah 4, 5, 19, 45, 94
Silicon Valley 98
Singapore 1, 5, 6
situatedness 30, 31, 47
Skype 107
skyscraper 1, 101, 107, 114
slavery 100
slum 9, 14, 81–3, 86, 92, 101, 114, 118, 129n2
smart city 1, 2, 4–8, 17, 20, 47, 48, 73, 76, 90, 95, 97, 100–1, 107, 114, 121, 124
smart grid 23, 25
smartphone 6, 7, 34–6, 44–5, 61, 80, 97, 107
Snap Scan 62, 124
social justice 13, 19, 72, 86, 118
Social Justice Coalition 86, 118
social media 2, 12–14, 19, 23, 27, 43, 51, 61, 62, 65, 68, 71–7, 80, 81, 86, 91, 99, 115–19, 124
  see also Facebook, Instagram, social networking, Twitter
social networking 18, 39, 53, 62, 71, 112
socio-technical 3, 4, 7, 10–17, 21, 29–32, 34, 40, 44, 46–8, 80, 89, 90, 109, 116, 121–4
software 22, 23, 30, 44, 65, 92, 102, 128n19
Soko Afya 56
Soko Yethu 54–5
solidarity 38, 50, 61

South Africa 2, 5, 12, 19, 20, 27, 35, 44, 46, 50–3, 57–60, 68, 69, 72, 73, 83, 86, 90, 99, 106, 113–18, 120, 123
  platform urbanism 16, 20, 21, 25, 34, 43, 107, 109–11, 121
  see also Cape Town, Durban
Soviet 67
spaza shop 57, 58, 60, 68, 113, 115, 123
stability 9, 68, 97, 111
stakeholder 5, 9, 76, 79, 81–3, 93
start-up 27, 42, 57
state oppression 110
stereotype 67
storytelling 14, 19, 27, 61, 71, 77, 79, 99, 100, 120
street vendor 1, 24, 52, 53, 57, 112
student 66, 97, 99, 107, 120
subaltern 2, 8, 37, 101, 125
sub-Saharan 6, 7
supermarket 36, 49, 52, 57, 64, 112, 124
surveillance 23, 34, 35
sustainable development goals (SDGs) 70
Swahili 37, 41, 66

T

Tanzania 13, 46, 67, 84, 117
  see also National Bureau of Statistics, Zanzibar
taxi 11, 24, 33, 41–2, 102
  see also BebaBeba, *boda-boda*, Bolt, Lyft, *matatus*, ride-hailing, rideshare, Uber
Taxify *see* Bolt
technoscience 31, 46, 130
Techweez 42
telecommunications 18, 19, 31, 40, 97, 106
television 71, 82, 124
Time magazine 83
tourism 36, 41, 43, 66, 73
traffic 5, 11, 36, 38–40, 45, 47, 102, 111–12
  control 112
transport 9, 11, 24, 33, 34, 45, 52–4, 57, 58, 74, 101–2, 112, 114, 117
Treatment Action Campaign 72, 120
trolling 62, 79, 119
trust 8, 11, 16, 38, 54, 61, 79, 81, 109, 118–21
Tunisia 71
Twiga 12, 49, 50–5, 56, 57, 65, 68, 110–16, 118, 119, 122–4, 127n2–8
Twitter 42, 74, 79, 120, 124, 127n6

U

Uber 3, 11, 19, 35–40, 41, 44, 45, 62, 88, 127n5
Uganda 2, 11, 24, 27, 32, 33, 45, 48, 52, 53, 88, 119, 122
Unequal Scenes 83, 120
  see also Miller, Johnny

145

United Cities and Local Governments of
    Africa (UCLG-A) 81
United Nations (UN) 8, 84
    Global Compact Action Guide 84
    Human Settlements Programme (UN
        Habitat) 8
unmanned aerial vehicles (UAV) 66
urbanism 2–9, 10, 16–21, 25, 28, 29, 31, 46,
    86, 88, 91, 100, 101, 106–10, 112, 115,
    116, 120, 121, 124
    pedagogical 73
    platform 3, 4, 16, 18, 20, 21, 25, 34, 43–6,
        86, 88, 91, 106–10, 112, 115, 116, 121
    smart 2, 6, 9, 10, 19–21, 29, 85, 109, 120
urban
    dweller 5, 7, 9, 19, 26, 64, 71
    planning 24, 28, 64, 71, 88
urbanization 4–9, 12, 50, 66
Ushahidi 92

V

vendor 1, 12, 24, 27, 37, 48, 50–7, 60, 63,
    68, 112, 122–4
violence 39, 92, 110
Vision 2030 5, 95, 96
voucher 62, *63*, 124

W

water 5, 20, 23–5, 45, 51, 53, 101–2
    meter 23, 25

see also sanitation
ways of working 61, 62, 79, 115, 119,
    123, 124
Web 2.0 21
well-being 70
Western Cape 60, 75, 128n2
Western Cape Economic Development
    Partnership (WCEDP) 60
Western Cape High Court 75
WhatsApp 12–14, 61–5, 68, 77, 79, 82, 113,
    118, 119, 123, 124
wholesale 52, 53
Wi-Fi 95, 96
Wikipedia 92
women 13, 44, 54, 67, 92, 94, 102
Woodstock 74–5
workforce 43, 67
World Bank 66, 67
worlding 10, 71
World Urban Forum 73, 81, 83

Y

Yebo Fresh 54, 57–8, *59*, 68, 110, 123
YouTube *64*, 71, 92, 123

Z

Zanzibar 13, 51, 66–8, 108, 111, 117
    Mapping Initiative 66–7
Zoom 113

www.ingramcontent.com/pod-product-compliance
Lightning Source LLC
Chambersburg PA
CBHW071208070526
44584CB00019B/2960